M000194659

Imaginal Preaching

AN ARCHETYPAL PERSPECTIVE

James A. Wallace

PAULIST PRESS
New York/Mahwah, N.J.

Credit to James A. Wallace and Lawrence Boadt for photographs in this book.

Cover design by Christine Taylor, Wilsted & Taylor Publishing Services, Inc.

Copyright © 1995 by the Redemptorists

All rights reserved. No part of this book may be reproduced or transmitted in any form or by any means, electronic or mechanical, including photocopying, recording or by any information storage and retrieval system without permission in writing from the Publisher.

Library of Congress Cataloging-in-Publication Data

Wallace, James A., 1944-
    Imaginal preaching : an archetypal perspective / James A. Wallace.
        p.   cm.
    Includes bibliographical references and index.
    ISBN 0-8091-3557-4 (alk. paper)
    1. Preaching. 2. Image (Theology) 3. Archetype (Psychology)
I. Title.
BV4211.2.W275 1995   94-46297
251—dc20   CIP

Published by Paulist Press
997 Macarthur Blvd.
Mahwah, N.J. 07430

Printed and bound in the
United States of America

Contents

To Lee Zahner-Roloff
friend and mentor

By Way of a Foreword

How we think about the speaking event tells us as much about ourselves as the culture in which we are reared and nurtured. If we conceive the speaking event as *rhetorical*, our energies are directed to all or several of the following: to persuade, to convince, to exhort, in short, to move a person to have a "concept," "product," "conviction," as close to the speaker's as possible, or better yet, to have a belief system identical to the speaker. The long and the short of the rhetorical model is that there is a sensed reaction of success or failure, of win or loss, of achievement or lack of it. *Powerful speakers* have vast audiences, largely already convinced of the speaker's beliefs and system of thought. There is nowhere to go with this model. These speakers are "charismatic," "solid," "logical," "thrilling." It is, in short, something of a star-system model. It is an ego-driven model; it is, virtually, our "cultural favorite," if the truth be known. It is also, and lamentably for the religious speaker, something of a "royalty of the mountain" phenomenon, leaving those less blessed with these formidable skills located in a speaker's purgatory.

What if there were another model for the speaker of soul, a model that is not based upon the rhetoric of persuasion, but is, rather, centered upon the psychological experience common to humankind? This model would be *revelatory*, *imaginal*, and *psychological*. It is this model that Father James Wallace explores in this astonishingly vital and inspiring book, *Imaginal Preaching*. Based upon the analytical psychology of Carl Gustav Jung and the archetypal psychology of James Hillman, *Imaginal Preaching* validates the persistence of image and its integrity as the alternative to rhetoric. It approaches preaching as *poesis*, an act of making, shaping, and forming *of*—and by—images.

In the summer of 1993, I had the opportunity to explore the con-

1

structs and explorations of Father Wallace's text with pastors enrolled in the Association of Chicago Theological Schools' Doctor of Ministry in Preaching Program. From the intensity of personal experience, I know the power Father Wallace's contribution can make to the education of preachers. Teaching from the text which follows simply reorganized and reoriented experienced preachers allowing, as one put it, "...to experience for the first time not only my own religious images, but the authority of these images that originate from my own soul." The restoration of "soul" to the "preaching event" must be experienced as a full extension of one of Jung's favorite phrases: *dixi et animam salvavi* ("I spoke and saved my own soul").

Lee Zahner-Roloff
Professor Emeritus, Northwestern University
Training Analyst, C.G. Jung Institute of Chicago
August, 1993

Introduction

Twenty years ago I read James Hillman's *Insearch: Psychology and Religion* and came across these words: "the cultivation of one's own world of image and mood, of feeling and fantasy, of one's own garden, is essential for what might be called the religious moment."[1] At the time I had just completed my first year of teaching homiletics in a Roman Catholic seminary in upstate New York. My own limited experience in preaching had convinced me that what engaged me as I was preaching and what seemed to engage my listeners were such imaginal realities as metaphor and story. Hillman's call to cultivate the world of image because of its importance for "the religious moment" rang true. And it seemed to me that his work would have relevance for preachers.

Over the years I have continued to read and reflect on Hillman's work and have become convinced of the importance he attaches to the work of "soul-making" and its implications for the preaching task. My earliest memories of religion had given me an awareness of the importance of my soul. I had grown up with the belief that the goal of life was to save my soul and was first drawn to ministry as a calling that helped others to save their souls. While not relinquishing this traditional understanding, my appreciation for ministry has broadened. Furthermore, Hillman has provided me with a further way to think about this work of caring for soul, one rooted in a psycho-spiritual appreciation for the cultivation of the imagination.

Chapter 1 begins by considering the role that images play in our lives, especially in the everyday life that preaching addresses. Images are also recognized as central to preaching. First, attention will be given to some images *of* preaching. The preacher can act out of a variety of images that shed light on preaching and offer various understandings of this language event—for instance, the image of the preacher as teacher or witness, as interpreter or herald. These different images direct preaching toward certain distinct ends whose importance depends on

the present state and needs of the community. Second, we will attend to
the importance of images *within* preaching. Preachers have recently
come to a renewed respect for the important role that imagery plays in
preaching. The choice of the image that will be the "heart" of a homily
is not to be taken lightly.

Chapter 2 will provide an introduction to the thought of James
Hillman, distilled from his writings on archetypal psychology. We will
focus especially on his understanding of the soul/psyche and its relation
to the imaginal world. Hillman's thought will be approached first as a
source for some general guidelines to assist the preacher in cultivating
the images entrusted to us, located both in the biblical texts and in various other resources of the Judaeo-Christian religious tradition. Of particular interest for the approach taken here is Hillman's insight that the
classical myths with their figures of Greek divinities offer ways of
thinking about the soul and its images. Certain mythic figures offer
preachers viable metaphors for imagining *how* images interact with
both the individual and communal consciousness, engaging mind, heart,
and will in distinct ways according to the different archetypal pattern
embodied in each myth.

Chapter 3 will then offer the Eros-Psyche myth as a paradigm for the
preacher's engagement with an imaginal text, that is, any text in which
images are found, whether explicitly or implicitly. By considering the
biblical text as Eros in relation to the preacher's Psyche, we can imagine every engagement with a text as a re-enactment of this myth. The
different stages of the myth can be seen as recapitulated in the preacher's interaction with a text recognized as having its own subjectivity.
Just as Psyche must undergo a series of trials to achieve union with
Eros, so must the preacher submit to the tasks that can awaken his or
her soul and bring it into a new relationship with the text. It is only by
this achieved union with the imaginal biblical text that the preacher can,
in turn, offer the text to a community in a life-giving and evocative way.

Chapters 4, 5, and 6 offer three distinct ways in which an image can
be worked with, or, better yet, played with. The mythic figures of
Apollo, Dionysus, and Hermes will serve to name and embody three
distinct modes of imaginal preaching, each offering a gestalt or pattern
that corresponds to how a preacher can approach and feature an image.
These patterns are embodiments of certain archetypal structures identi-

fied by C.G. Jung and Hillman. Of interest for preachers is that these modalities name three distinct ways that the *same* image can function in the communal consciousness of those gathered for worship.

Chapter 7 will offer briefly an example of how a particular imaginal text is open to the various archetypal modes discussed, and then conclude with some examples of "Imaginal Preaching." These homilies try to feature the image of the biblical text or of the liturgical occasion in a way that awakens, engages and enlivens the imagination of the community. A brief Epilogue will bring the work to a close, alluding to some possibilities for further development.

This work is the result of my engagement with the unique perspective I have found in archetypal psychology. Rooted in the insights of psychologist Carl Gustav Jung and philosopher Henri Corbin, this imaginative approach receives its most articulate expression in the work of James Hillman. I believe it offers preachers a unique lens to ponder their work with the life-giving images found in the Judaeo-Christian religious tradition.

This effort has come to print because of the support of many people. I am grateful to my colleagues in homiletics, particularly Robert P. Waznak, Thomas A. Kane, William Hammelman, Joan Delaplane, John Allyn Melloh, and other members of the Catholic Association of the Teachers of Homiletics for their encouragement over the years. A special word of gratitude to Richard Ward and Don Wardlaw for their provocative comments during the final stages of this work. I am also indebted to many students over the past two decades whose work has challenged me to enter more deeply into the mystery of preaching the gospel. I am blessed with the ongoing support of such fellow Redemptorists as Francis Gargani, Frank Skelly, Joseph Tizio, and Kevin O'Neil, and such friends as Toi Derricotte, Catherine Rourke, and Leslie Thayer who read parts of this manuscript in various stages of its development.

I would, in closing, like to single out three people without whom this book would never have been finished. The Talmud says that every person should do two things in life: acquire a teacher and choose a friend. Each person of this human trinity has combined these two roles in a unique way: Leland Zahner-Roloff first introduced me to the thought of Carl Jung and James Hillman in the summer of 1974; over the past two decades he has been a constant source of support and friendship in my life, serving as teacher, mentor, and guide. Edward J. Gilbert, C.Ss.R., has been one of the most important influences in my life as a Redemptorist priest, as one of my teachers during my theological education and as an encouraging friend and religious superior for the last twenty-five years. Philip A. Dabney, C.Ss.R., first came into my life in my first years of teaching and was one of those students who made it a joy to come into the classroom; ever since then, he has taught me the value and unexpected graces of a life-long friendship. To these three I am most deeply indebted.

1.

The Imaginal World and Preaching

Life's Images

Images come to us endlessly from the day and night worlds. I awake with dreams and fragments of dreams evanescing into the morning light. The clock radio's early morning news spills the day's first images into my ear. I open the newspaper to see the requisite front page imagery: the president meeting with a group of senators, the pope reaching out to touch the hands of two young people in Denver during the recent Youth Conference, and the bodies of two more victims of that neo-Boschian hell called Bosnia. Through the day I receive images from my drive to and from school and the routine of my life that falls in between. I turn on the TV later in the evening to see footage from the most recent crime scene in Washington, D.C., followed by clips from the world of athletes, and terminating with the electronic auguries of the weather map. This past weekend I was enchanted by the magical realism of the movie "Like Water for Chocolate." Tomorrow the mailman will bring Tina Brown's *New Yorker*, with its wonderful cover and sly cartoons, in addition to the daily package of junk mail catalogues. Images, images, images! They come so frequently that we are inured to their impact. Most of the time, they bombard us without really touching us. But not always.

Neil Postman has written that whereas in the past one of the purposes of education was to defend ourselves against the seduction of eloquence, today we need to figure out how to defend ourselves against the seduction of imagery.[1] The age of orality has given way to the age of

7

imagery and the news is not all good. TV images have been linked with violent behavior; movies have led to killings in the parking lot; private nightmares have led to public disasters. Images that nourish and enliven are more than equaled by those that deaden and desensitize.

As a preacher and a teacher of preachers I am interested in the recent attention being given to imagery, the imagination and such imaginal forms as poetry and story by people in the theological and pastoral areas of study. I am particularly fascinated by the turn that has taken place in the area of homiletics, which might be called the turn toward the imaginal. In the preaching courses I had during my time as a student in the seminary, the emphasis was on preaching as an act of instruction and persuasion and the emphasis was placed on sound, logical thinking, captured in the desire to formulate your thought in one clear sentence, with appropriate rhetorical embellishments, so that you might join the ranks of "popular preachers" who did not bore their listeners. While only a few each generation were termed "giants of the pulpit," one hoped to be a worthy servant of the word of God. Recent developments, however, signal a change in this ideal of preaching as an act of rhetorical excellence to a perception of preaching as an act of imaginative theology.[2] Rhetoric, the art of persuasion, has given way to poesis, the art of making or shaping with words. Images have attained at least a parity with concepts.

The importance of the imaginal life in a community has been sounded from many different quarters. John Coleman, a Roman Catholic theologian, writes that "a people prospers only when it lives out of richly textured communal symbols and achieves its own unique sense of history, heroes and collective story."[3] In a country where a faithful group of people flood into Graceland every August 16, carrying candles and images of "the King," and where a greater number of people continuously visit the eternal flame that marks the grave of John F. Kennedy in Arlington National Cemetery and the black wall rising out of the earth that honors those killed in Vietnam, can anyone deny a need for heroes and a hunger for participation in the symbolic and ritual life? However, looking at our own society and the Catholic Church as part of that society, Coleman concludes that "today, however, Catholic America, like the larger nation, is a land without adequate symbols."[4]

In a similar vein, there is Robert Bellah's *Habits of the Heart*[5] with its diagnosis that the people of this country have increasingly become restricted to one shared "language," that of radical individualism. Our vocabulary has shrunk to a world view that is too narrowly focused. *Self-*consciousness is in danger of becoming the only consciousness. Bellah reminds us that in our common everyday speech we have practically lost two other "dialects" that we once possessed, the language of the biblical tradition and the language of republicanism, both rooted in an awareness of community, commitment, and the common good. Both were also highly imaginal languages. We still hear remnants of them in the call to be "that shining city on the hill" or to form a "new covenant," and in dutiful references to Lady Liberty and 4th of July appeals to justice, freedom, and equality. But the lack of these rich imaginal dialects of our past has impoverished us as a society, limiting our ability to articulate a life-giving vision. In addition to the community's social need for symbol and image, Mircea Eliade has called our attention to the fact that "the symbol, the myth, and the image are of the very substance of the spiritual life; they may become disguised, mutilated, or degraded, but are never extirpated."[6] The revival of such symbolic and mythical figures as the warrior, the mystic, the king, and the wild man in the men's movement and the recovery of the images of the goddess, the wise woman, and the woman who runs with the wolves in the women's movement point to the need within the human spirit for the imaginal realm.

Symbols, myths, and images, then, are of great importance to us on multiple levels, both on the individual and corporate as well as the spiritual and political. The imaginal realm carries with it the capacity to heal and to illuminate, to purify and to instruct, to unite and to empower. The concern of this book is to consider some of the ways in which preachers can work with the images and symbols of our religious tradition and our lives so that the imaginal realm might continue to function within the consciousness of both individuals and communities, strengthening identity and motivating action in the world.

In his play *Translations*, the Northern Ireland playwright Brian Friel has one of his characters say "it is not the literal past, the 'facts' of history that shape us, but images of the past embodied in language...we must never cease renewing those images, because once we do, we fossilize."[7] The images of the past can continue to provide self-definition and awareness and to remind us of the ongoing power of imagination to call us into the future. Such images are to be found in the biblical story and in the rich imagery of the Judaeo-Christian tradition. Images such as the garden, the new heaven and earth, the banquet, bread and wine, oil poured over the head, tears washing feet, fire from above, a newborn infant, and a crucified figure are only some of the ones that continue to throb with numinous power. The task of the preacher is to recover and renew them for the present generation and those to come, so that they are not lost in the mindless haze of imagery substituted by modern technology. Images will continue to be cast and sown into the field of human consciousness; the issue is which of them will take root and flower.

Preaching's Images

"Preaching's images" is an ambiguous phrase. We can understand it either as images *of* preaching or images *in* preaching. Both are pertinent here. First, we will consider images *of* preaching. In workshops for preachers I have asked participants to think of an image that captures each one's understanding of preaching. If a single image had to be chosen at this moment, what would it be? Some of the responses have been provocative. A breeze. A flame. A friend. One who nurtures. Someone who walks with the community. And, somewhat hesitatingly, an exhibitionist! The images we choose for ourselves can be very enlightening.

Such images provide identification for the preacher and assist our understanding of who we are and what we are trying to do when we preach. Thomas Long, professor of preaching at Princeton, says that "preachers have at least tacit images of the preacher's role, primary metaphors that not only describe the nature of the preacher but also embrace by implication all the other crucial aspects of the preaching event."[8] The image we are operating out of when we preach determines the kind of preaching our people will hear because it leads us to highlight certain tasks of preaching and to minimize others. The images we choose can challenge, encourage, or renew our call to preach. We will now consider a few that have been handed down to us.

1. THE HERALD

On December 4, 1963, the Second Vatican Council of the Roman Catholic Church issued its first document, the "Constitution on the Sacred Liturgy," as the first step in renewing its liturgical life. The document states that "the sermon...should draw its content mainly from scriptural and liturgical sources, for it is *the proclamation of God's wonderful works in the history of salvation*, which is the mystery of Christ ever made present and active in us, especially in the celebration of the liturgy."[9] We find here one of the earliest images of the preacher as one who proclaims God's wonderful works, past and present, that is, the herald. This proclamation of the gospel to all is designated the "primary duty" of bishops and priests in a later document.[10]

The image of the herald points the preacher toward the explicit proclamation of the good news of Jesus Christ, of the salvation that has been effected through his saving life, death, and resurrection. Just as the herald was the one that the king sent to proclaim to the people that the battle had been won and the enemies had been overcome, so too the preacher as herald. Furthermore, it is the herald's task to proclaim the risen Jesus "ever made present and active in us." In *Thinking in Story*, theologian Richard A. Jensen speaks of proclamation as the primary discourse of the church, characterized by an immediacy that is present-tense, person-to-person, and unconditional in its authority. Jensen emphasizes the herald as one who speaks for Christ at this moment when he says, "We speak on Christ's behalf. We don't talk about what Christ said long ago. We don't talk about Christ. We speak for Christ. Christ speaks through us."[11]

The image of the herald stresses God's activity through the herald for the sake of the listeners. The herald's task is to communicate the message that has been given. While the emphasis is especially on what God has done in the past, "God's wonderful works in the history of salvation," still the herald proclaims a saving action that is occurring in the present. This image gives weight to the transcendent dimension of preaching by emphasizing the preacher as an instrument that is picked up and played by God.

2. THE TEACHER

I would propose that the preacher as teacher was the dominant image accepted by Roman Catholicism from the time of the Council of Trent in the sixteenth century until the Second Vatican Council. We can hear this emphasis in the words decreed by Trent during its fifth session:

Archbishops, priests, and all who in any manner have charge of parochial and other churches to which is attached the *cura ani-*

marum (the care of souls), shall at least on Sundays and solemn
festivals, either personally or, if they are lawfully impeded, through
others who are competent, feed the people committed to them with
wholesome words in proportion to their own and their people's
mental capacity, by teaching them those things that are necessary
for all to know in order to be saved, and by impressing upon them
with briefness and plainness of speech the vices that they must
avoid and the virtues that they must cultivate, in order that they
may escape eternal punishment and obtain the glory of heaven.[12]

In its call for reform, Trent turned to preaching that would instruct people
in knowledge of the faith and in the behavior flowing from such knowledge. Catechesis and parenesis were its goals; the teacher its image.

This same image can also be found in the teaching of the Second
Vatican Council. In the same "Constitution on the Sacred Liturgy" quoted above, we hear that "by means of the homily the mysteries of the
faith and the guiding principles of the Christian life are expounded from
the sacred text."[13] Such statements retain and re-echo the emphasis found
in Paul's admonition to "hold to the standard of sound teaching" (2 Tim
1:13) and "teach what is consistent with sound doctrine" (Tit 2:1).

The preacher's task as teacher goes beyond conveying information;
he or she offers an understanding of the faith that illuminates the life of
the community and guides its action in the world. William J. Carl stresses this function of preaching when he says that "believers suffer from a
theological identity crisis, and...it is the church's role to help people
discover who they are as Christians.... When people do not know what
they believe, they cannot be expected to worship, nurture, or go into the
world ministering and acting in Christ's name."[14] It is one of preaching's
major tasks to uncover the relevance and implications of church teaching for listeners' lives. In our age when theological literacy is becoming
less and less a presumption and more a surprise, the preacher's role as
teacher may once again assume a greater importance and be considered
a central aspect to the preacher's identity as pastor.[15]

3. THE WITNESS

In 1975, a decade after the Second Vatican Council, Pope Paul VI
wrote in his exhortation "On Evangelization in the Modern World" that
"modern man listens more willingly to witnesses than to teachers, and

if he does listen to teachers, it is because they are witnesses."[16] This document locates the church's activity of providing living witness—"the witness of poverty and detachment, of freedom in the face of the powers of this world, in short, the witness of sanctity"[17]—as key to the evangelization of the world.

The importance of the witness in the life of the church can be traced back to the apostolic church. The Acts of the Apostles begins with the risen Lord telling his disciples that "you will be my witnesses in Jerusalem, in all Judea and Samaria, and to the ends of the earth" (Acts 1:8). While the call to witness is directed to every Christian, this image has special resonance for the preacher.

Thomas G. Long makes this figure central to his theological vision of preaching in *The Witness of Preaching*.[18] He acknowledges that even though the witness has been linked both with certain aggressive forms of evangelism and with the not always edifying legal arena, still this image provides a unique emphasis to the preaching task with its two central characteristics: "the witness has seen something and is willing to tell the truth about it."[19] The role of witness calls a preacher to give testimony to a truth that he or she has known, demanding that the witness' life be lived in accordance with this truth, because this truth is founded in the mystery that is God.

The preacher as witness has seen God's presence and heard God's voice in the scripture and is willing to stake his or her life on it. Long emphasizes that the preacher does not lay claim to authority on the basis of greater Christian experience than the people addressed, nor to any greater share of wisdom or common sense or theological knowledge. But the preacher is "the one whom the congregation sends on their behalf, week after week to the scripture," listening for God's presence and claim.[20] The preacher goes to meet God in the scriptures, to hear God speaking to *us*; the preacher goes to meet God precisely as one of us, a member of the community and of the world, taking the questions and concerns of the community. Scripture is the meeting ground where Christ addresses the church and it is the witness who testifies to this.

4. THE INTERPRETER

A final image of the preacher comes from one of the most recent documents of the Roman Catholic tradition. Sponsored by the National

Conference of Catholic Bishops, the Bishops' Committee on Priestly Life and Ministry addresses preachers in the document *Fulfilled in Your Hearing: The Homily in the Sunday Assembly* (hereafter *FIYH*), which offers a paradigm shift for Roman Catholic preachers as they approach preaching during the Sunday liturgical celebrations of the church. Rather than giving priority to the role of teacher, the expositor of the saving mysteries and guiding principles of Christian life, the document points in a different direction by selecting the image of the interpreter.

The Second Vatican Council had stated that the homily was "to be highly esteemed as part of the liturgy itself";[21] indeed, a later liturgical instruction calls it "an integral part of the liturgical action."[22] The use of the word "integral" reminds preachers that the preaching is part of the whole of the particular liturgical action. It is the link between the liturgy of the word and the liturgy of the eucharist, providing the motivation for the community to lift up their hearts in thanks and praise. This particular awareness led to the understanding found in *FIYH*, which defines a liturgical homily in the following way: "a scriptural interpretation of human existence which enables a community to recognize God's active presence, to respond to that presence in faith through liturgical word and gesture, and beyond the liturgical assembly, through a life lived in conformity with the Gospel."[23]

This understanding of the homily as an interpretive act makes it distinct from preaching that proclaims the basic kerygma or preaching that is instructive in faith and morals. The focus is not primarily on what God *has* done, nor on the teaching of saving mysteries and the cultivation of virtue, but on offering a way to understand the life of the community as the arena of God's presence and ongoing activity. And the primary instrument employed to arrive at such an understanding is the biblical text. The interpreter is the mediator of meaning, the one who moves in the "between," standing between scripture texts and people, between the tradition of living belief and contemporary life, and between the living God revealed in Jesus of Nazareth and the body of Christ gathered for worship in the power of the Spirit.

Throughout the document, the preacher-interpreter is spoken of in ways that further our understanding of what this role implies. As a mediator of meaning, the preacher is a listener who hears both the biblical word and the words of those present in the assembly, words that question, doubt, and challenge, words spoken in anger, confusion, and hurt, and words uttered in joy, love, and an awareness of the graciousness of life. The interpreter re-presents in the preaching act both the living God and the community of faith, connecting revelation, life, and liturgy, and pointing to the presence of God in the present. Through this activity the interpreter enables the community to give thanks in the liturgy of the eucharist and, beyond that, to live a life "in conformity with the Gospel."

What makes this image of particular interest is the emphasis on the locus of revelation. The interpreter focuses on God's revealing action *now* in the lives of this community; the scripture is a means for recognizing this. The images of herald, teacher, and witness stress the revelation that is found in the text or in the tradition and then is applied to the present; the interpreter takes very seriously God's living presence in the experience of *these* people in *this* place at *this* time.

Herald, teacher, witness, interpreter. All four images are foundational to the task of preaching, each drawing us toward a particular aspect of the gospel mandate. They are reminders that preachers live out of self-understandings rooted in the imaginal world. Preachers need to reflect and meditate on these and other new images that come from their experience of what the preaching ministry embodies. But, as important as the images *of* preaching are for the preacher's self-understanding, so too the images *in* preaching contribute to that of the believing community.

Images in Preaching

My earliest memories of preaching have to do with the stories I heard. Some forty years later I still remember Father Doetzler, a very old priest in my memory (now I know he was in his 50s!), who often spoke to the school children on special occasions. He talked to us in stories. I didn't realize the importance of what he was doing at the time, but when I came across one of the first books on narrative preaching twenty-five years later, I had no difficulty appreciating what the authors wrote:

> Most people try to connect their smaller stories to a larger one; there is hardly a tribe in the world that does not ritualize the significant events of the human story in a way which ties them to the

processes of nature and the rhythm of the universe. It is the same
in the church. At our baptism we enter into a story, a very large
one; call it The Story.... Our stories merge with The Story, find
their meaning in that coalescence, and if we allow it, renew the
telling of The Story.[24]

"Narrative preaching" as an area of study that concentrates on the
interweaving of God's story, the people's story, and the preacher's story
dates from the early 1980s. Since *Preaching the Story* by Steimle, et al.,
many other works have deepened our awareness of how narrative structures, attention to characters, an appreciation for the narrative quality of
our life, and other literary and oral qualities can benefit preaching.[25] The
area of narrative preaching has contributed greatly to shifting the
approach of homiletics from a discursive, analytic enterprise to a more
inductive, experiential one.

Most recently, attention has begun to shift from narrative as a heuris-
tic device toward a focus on the role of imagination and images in
preaching. Story, of course, can be seen as a type of extended imaginal
experience, in which images are sequentially related and given greater
definition by their context within a narrative. Often a story is the carrier
of a particular image that sticks in one's memory, bearing with it
thought, feeling, mood, and a potential to motivate in proportion to its
ability to touch the depths of one's being. Such an image can become
the focus of prolonged meditation and reflection.

The concern with image has led to a renewed interest in the imagination. In his provocative work, *Imagining God*,[26] Garrett Green treats the
imagination as *the* locus for revelation. He proposes the imagination as
the primary arena in which God works and plays to reveal God's self.
From this perspective, Green proposes that God impressed the divine
image, embodied in Jesus Christ, on the first witnesses who, in turn,
gave expression to it in the gospels. The gospels in turn continue to
impress themselves on our minds and hearts. This flow of images into
human consciousness takes place especially in the reading and preaching of the gospel.

Rubem Alves asks, "Did you know that images have the power to
possess those who see them?"[27] And also those who hear them. For
preachers and listeners, images are more than verbal decorations, or lit-
erate divertissements, more than attention-getters or -holders. "The

more we turn to the picture language of the poet and the storyteller, the more we will be able to preach in a way that invites people to respond from the heart as well as from the mind."[28]

How can we think about the working of the imagination and the different ways in which images grasp and move us? Contemporary homileticians have been reflecting in terms of the direction in which images can lead a community. Elizabeth Achtemeier writes that "if we want to change someone's life from non-Christian to Christian, from dying to living, from despairing to hoping, from anxious to certain, from corrupted to whole, we must change the images, the imaginations of the heart."[29] There is the sense here of image's power to effect the deepest change that is possible, a change in life orientation, the theological journey of conversion. Images, in this framework, work in the depths of our beings and allow us to burrow more deeply into the mystery of God.

Another direction is named by Thomas Troeger when he says that "we preachers need to build our sermons so that our listeners can step securely from image to image, from story to story, and thus climb up into the truths of their lives."[30] For Troeger, the preacher is a weaver of images, knitting verbal ladders to assist an upward climb. The preacher's use of images allows for an ascent into union with Truth. Through the images offered, communal ascent is possible.

Walter Brueggemann's vision in *Finally Comes the Poet* reminds us of image's capacity to move us outward. It is the poet who speaks words that embody an alternative vision of reality. The poet gives us another world to enter. The poet's image of a new world evokes what Brueggemann calls a "transformed obedience." By transforming those places of resistance able to be overcome "only by stories, images, metaphor and phrases that live out the world differently," the poet uses imaginal language that will only come to fruition in the re-creation of the outer world.[31]

A final voice that witnesses to image's great power in our lives is found in some of the last words written by William Lynch, a Roman Catholic theologian whose life work was rooted in the appreciation of the imagination. In an article that appeared shortly before his death, he wrote that "it may well be that we shall be finally judged by our images as much as by any other factor in the human condition. So full of thought and choice and freedom are they. Or so empty that they are inhuman."[32] The impact of this statement comes home when one considers how our predominantly masculine images of God have conditioned not only how we think about and relate to the One who called us into being, but also have been determinative of how power and authority have been used and abused in our world and our church.[33]

Images work. They work for us, against us, in us, and through us. They can transform us in our depths, move us toward the highest truth, motivate us to change the world, and ultimately influence the final outcome when we stand face to face with our God. These are no mean claims. "Do you not know that images have the power to possess those who see them?" It is said that hearing is the most intimate sense, because the words that come from the interior of one person enter into the deepest parts of another and can remain there for a lifetime. Preaching operates in this interior realm. Do you not know that images have the power to possess those who *hear* them?

Imaginal preaching calls for a particular way of approaching our task. Rather than looking for the main idea, the key thought, we search for the dominant image in the story, the letter, the prophetic word, that image which will control all that we say, that will serve thought, feeling and motivation. Imaginal preaching also calls us to attend to the images that we are given by life and by the faith tradition we serve; but it is most important that we first look and listen attentively to those found in the primary sources for preaching, the biblical texts. The liturgical theologian Mark Searle pointed in this direction when he wrote:

> The texts of Scripture and images of liturgy are not didactic messages wrapped up in some decorative covering which can be thrown away when the content is extracted. They are images and sets of images to be toyed with, befriended, rubbed over and over again, until gradually and sporadically, they yield flashes of insight and encounter with the "Reality" of which they sing. Their purpose is not to give rise to thought (at least not immediately), but to mediate encounter. [34]

Such an approach is playful, intimate, personal, and profoundly serious, calling us to relate to the text and the liturgical image not as an object to be broken open and plundered but an "other" to be engaged and honored, reverentially touched and cherished.

We approach the scriptures for their images and bring them into relationship with the life of our community and the larger world. What happens when a dominant image of the text—be it a character, a moment in the story, or a key metaphor—is set over against some aspect of our lives? Such is the concern of this work. The preacher is to see himself or herself as situated in the realm of the "between." The preacher moves back and forth, a citizen of two realms, a mediator of meaning, a custodian of metaphor.

FIYH calls preachers to "dwell in the word." This is an invitation to immerse oneself in the world of the text. But one takes the plunge in order to realize another exhortation: "the homily is not so much *on* the scriptures as *from* and *through* them."[35] The homily is not so much an explanation of the scriptures as a process of first entering their world (thus speaking *from* them) and then using this world as a lens to look out onto our world (thereby speaking *through* them).

Images surround and constantly clamor for our attention. Periodically one takes up root in our lives in a way that bears fruit again and again. This fruit can be healthy or poisonous. The preacher can make a contribution to the faith life of the community by offering images that seed the community's imagination. The preacher will set before the community images from the text that are sometimes set in tension with images from the ongoing life of the community. Sometimes the text challenges life, but life can also challenge the text. Or images are offered that can be contemplated for their own sake, either as characters that can live with us, or a moment in a story that resonates and illumines our experiences.

We have considered the constant presence of images in our lives, and the importance of images for preaching, both for the preacher's identity and for the community's growth in spirit and truth. Questions and concerns arise. Of particular concern is how preachers can work with images that have been part of our collective lives for so long. Images can dry up and die in their ability to influence, to flow meaningfully into our lives. Is there a way of renewing them? Also, homileticians provocatively indicate that images work on us in different ways, taking us in different directions. Is there a way of deliberately crafting an image to "move" us in a certain direction? How do we grow in our appreciation for the image as something living, with its own subjectivity?

I would like to turn now to the thought of archetypal psychologist

James Hillman who has articulated the importance of image for what he considers life's primary vocation, "the making of soul." The stimulating psychological perspective found in Hillman's work can provide a unique perspective for preachers desiring to work with images and to allow images to work with them.

2.

The Soul's Language: Images and the Archetypal World of James Hillman

"We humans are primarily acts of imagination, images."
James Hillman

Image Begets Image

Two years ago my cousin Karen died of cancer. She was still in her early forties and left behind her husband, Gary, and her four year old son, Joey. After she died at the hospital, I went with Gary and Karen's two brothers to her parents' home where Joey was staying. Joey did not know his mother had died. Gary and Karen's father took Joey back into the bedroom. After a moment, there was a cry, more a howl, of pain. It pierced the heart. Then there was silence. Not too long after, they returned to the room where the rest of us were sitting. Joey went over to the video and started to play a game. After a few moments, he looked up and asked,

"Why did Mom die?"

"Because she was very sick. She had cancer," Gary answered.

21

"Oh," Joey replied and went back to the game.

Then, "Where is she now?"

"She's in heaven with God."

Again silence for a few moments.

Then, "How did she get there?"

"Two angels came for her and took her."

Again, silence.

Finally, "What did they look like?"

Six adults glanced helplessly at each other.

Then, "They were beautiful," Gary said.

Joey looked away and slowly nodded.

To speak in images is to speak to the soul. As Joey was given each answer, I could see him stop and think about it, before he went on to the next question. It was like watching rain soaking into the soil. The answers came simply, in images that a child could understand and absorb.

Carl Jung once wrote that image *is* psyche. James Hillman has written in a similar vein that psyche is constituted of images, that images are the stuff of psyche. For both of them images were the central manifestation of "esse in anima," that is, "to be in soul." This chapter will consider the thought of James Hillman as it is found in his writings on archetypal psychology. This is not simply a psychology of archetypes, those primordial patterns that can be found in dreams, literature, and life. But, as Thomas Moore, points out, "the idea is to see every fragment of life and every dream as myth and poetry."[1] Archetypal psychology attunes us to the importance of the images in our lives, those coming to us in our dreams, in the art and literature of the past, and those that surround us in our everyday lives; it invites us to consider them as manifestations of soul.

This is a different way of thinking about soul. For most of us, soul is the innermost aspect of the human person, the spiritual principle that informs us, truly animating us and enabling our self-understanding as women and men formed in the image of God. As I mentioned earlier, I was brought up in a faith tradition that put great emphasis on "saving one's soul." But in the world of archetypal psychology, soul is identified not with spirit but with the sphere of psyche, and psyche is connected with imagination and heart. The care of the soul has to do with tending and cultivating the images that come to us from the depths of our own souls and those of others who have left them in our custodial care. Such images are the thought of the heart.

Since preachers are the primary caretakers of the images of the Judaeo-Christian tradition, Hillman's work can be most provocative, for it provides a way of thinking about what we are doing in our efforts to craft homilies that are both biblically grounded and experientially relevant to the lives of people living into the twenty-first century. In this chapter we will look at Hillman's understanding of soul and its imaginal expressions and consider some of the ways he proposes for living "soul-full" lives.

The Soul and Soul-Making

In an early work on religion and psychology, *Insearch*,[2] Hillman gives a telling anecdote about an elderly woman confined to a wheelchair in a sanatarium in Zurich and suffering a deep inner isolation. One day she turned to the psychiatrist attending her and said, "I am dead because I have lost my heart." The doctor gently suggested that she put her hand over her breast and she would be certain to feel her heart beating. "That is not my real heart," the woman replied. A silence fell over the room as she and the psychiatrist looked at each other.

Hillman comments that the woman was indeed speaking the truth for she had lost "the loving courageous connection to life—and that is the real heart, not the ticker which can as well pulsate isolated in a glass bottle." It is this particular loss that Hillman refers to as the "loss of soul." For the realm of the heart is the realm of the soul, that inner region that links the person with the life force. This old woman was undergoing the same devastating experience that even our earliest ancestors had known.

The phrase "loss of soul" has been used to describe a condition anthropologists found among "primitive" peoples. In suffering this, a person felt unable to take part in society's rituals or traditions. One's link with family and nature was inexplicably gone. The only word to capture this was "death." A person was dead to what mattered most. Loss of soul was an experience of profound disconnectedness, both with the outer world of other human beings and the inner world at the depths of one's being. "Without this soul, [one] has lost the sense of

belonging and the sense of being in communion with the powers and
the gods," Hillman writes.[3] In such a state, a person is not sick with dis-
ease nor out of one's mind, but the condition is sufficiently serious that
physical death can result. Hillman's conclusion from the testimony both
of anthropologists and of people confined to psychiatric hospitals is that
we can and do lose our souls. Furthermore, such a loss is not restricted
to individuals; a culture, a society, any communal body of people, even
a congregation, can lose its soul.

What more can we understand about this soul whose loss proves to be
so devastating? Why is soul so important to the quality of a human life?
What does archetypal psychology as a psychology of soul have to contribute to its recovery? And, in terms of our interest, what does all this
have to do with preaching? Let us begin with Hillman's understanding
of the soul.

When Hillman speaks of the soul or psyche, he makes a point of dis-
tinguishing it from body and mind. Following the Neoplatonic tradition,
soul is said to be the first principle that functions between the body and
mind. Body is related to the world of matter and nature, the concrete
and the sensuous; mind is linked with the world of spirit, ideas, abstractions, concepts, and logic. For too long body and mind/spirit have been
considered the total reality of the human person. But psyche or soul is
the mid-ground between the senses on the one hand and cognition on
the other. Psyche or soul is the necessary perspective *between*, linking
the other two.

Like Caesar's Gaul, the human person is conceived as being tripar-
tite in the imaginal fantasy proposed by archetypal psychology. Its
anthropology is set against the traditional dualism of body and spirit.
Thus, the modern person has often been in search of soul, because it has
not been acknowledged as a distinct sphere of activity. For both Jung
and Hillman, the goal of life is "esse in anima" (to be in soul). And the
failure "to be in soul" necessitates the study (logos) of soul (psyche):
psychology. Another way to understand psychology would be as the
speech (logos) of soul (psyche); it is the field of study that encourages
the soul to speak, thereby providing an adequate account of itself.

And when we study the soul, what do we learn? When the soul
speaks, how can we recognize it? Hillman's understanding of the soul is
first given in broad strokes. He says that soul is "a perspective rather

than a substance, a viewpoint toward things rather than the thing itself."[4] Here he is taking care not to substantiate or reify soul; thus, it reveals itself as a perspective, a way of looking at things. Resisting all attempts to either define, literalize, limit, or simplify, Hillman's deliberately ambiguous concept nevertheless points toward soul as a distinctive ability, noting it as "that unknown human factor which makes meaning possible, which turns events into experiences, and which is communicated in love."[5] Such powers reveal soul as a force that connects us more deeply and fully with life. Furthermore, the soul has "a religious concern" and "a special relation with death." These latter aspects remind us of soul's link with the depths and the areas of ultimate concern. In his own work on the care of the soul, Thomas Moore writes that soul "has to do with depth, value, relatedness, heart and personal substance."[6]

But most telling for the preacher is Hillman's statement that soul is "the imaginative possibility in our natures, the experiencing through reflective speculation, dream, image and fantasy—that mode which recognizes all realities as primarily symbolic or metaphorical."[7] When Hillman says that soul allows our recognition of all life as "primarily symbolic or metaphorical," he invites us into the active cultivation of poetic vision which soul enables. Soul is identified with our imagining capability, since "images are the stuff of psyche." Soul-making, then, is explained as "a seeing or hearing by means of an imagining that sees through an event to its image."[8] This operation of seeing through an event, of hearing through an experience, to the image is at the heart of being "in soul."

An example of seeing through an event to its image might be helpful. A city had decided to put in a recreational lake. Hillman was called on as a consultant. To take this civic decision solely as an event would limit understanding of its import to its external aspect, restricting our comprehension to the desire of the population to provide a place to bring their children on weekends during the summer, a place for the senior citizens to gather in safety, a haven from exhaust fumes. This is fine as far as it goes; it is just that it does not go far enough.

For Hillman, such a plan says more when one thinks about it on the level of image, looking for and listening to its metaphorical, symbolic resonances; it speaks of the need of the community for moisture, of its desire for a place that relieves its parchedness. The community's soul needs a place to get "wet," a pool of reverie to relieve the dryness that can accompany either too much "spirit" or abstraction or too much body heat or materialism. Soul-making points us through the event, toward the image and is, therefore, a movement away from *only* the literal toward the metaphorical.

Such an operation leads Hillman to speak of the "poetic basis of mind," meaning that the best way to study the mind is through its images. He would understand the mind in relation to the imagination, rather than vice versa. Thus, psyche or soul is imagined as located between the perspective of body which would celebrate the physical reality of the lake, the embodiment of the image, and the mind which would conceive the plan to meet the recreational needs of the city and bring the image to fulfillment. The soul is to be found deep within the image, ever sensitive to the sounds of a symbol crashing.

Hillman also wishes to retrieve the notion of "*anima mundi*," the soul of the world. Soul is not to be limited to us humans but is in the world, in buildings, transportation, politics, economics, and so forth. When we deprive the world of soul, we render it inanimate, soul-less. It is this treatment that has brought us to such an ecological crisis; we treat everything apart from ourselves as objects to be freely disposed of. Archetypal psychology tries to unveil the images of the world, to allow each thing, living or not, to manifest its being. The soul of the world is "that particular soul-spark, that seminal image, which offers itself through each thing in its visible form, the sensuous presentation of each thing as a face bespeaking its interior image."[9] When we gaze upon the world and what is around us, we are looking into its soul.

Hillman takes very seriously that this world is the place of soul-making, calling us to honor the manifestations of soul that surround us in the world. "Call the world, if you please, 'the vale of Soul-making.' Then you will find out the use of the world," wrote John Keats. When we heed this advice, we may find the basis for "the religious moment" not only in the images that come in dream and fantasy but also that any world event is an occasion for cultivating soul. When we engage in soul-making, we release events from their literal understanding "in order to search out their shadowy, metaphorical significances for soul."

To be engaged in the task of soul-making will locate us in a different place than we usually function. So much of our lives is spent in the building up of the ego, the sense of "I," and coming to terms with the values and limits of a strong sense of personal consciousness. But soul-making takes us beyond this project and moves us to a place in which there is a recognition of our connection with a power greater than ego. Hillman wishes to replace what he calls the "heroic ego," that mode of consciousness that sees things from a single perspective, with what he calls an "imaginal ego."

The heroic ego is identified as the guiding influence of western civilization, the ego raised to overcome all obstacles, chop down the forest, conquer the beast, save the princess (or prince, if you will), and achieve the prize, be it kingdom or corporation. The heroic ego is behind scientific achievement and technological advance. Without it, we would not have achieved the scientific and technological advances that we now take for granted. Yet, it has the potential to function not only as savior but also as tyrant, imposing its way of seeing things, its perspective and will on all who come within its influence. The heroic ego tends to reduce everyone and everything to supporting status, and to see the rest of the world in a depersonalized way, as soul-less, at the service of itself.

In contrast, Hillman calls for an "imaginal ego," one that gives multiple perspectives, and many sources of meaning, direction, and value. An imaginal ego allows for soul's many faces and voices, each needing to be honored. Ego is just one perspective, one voice, and needs to know its relative importance. For Hillman, the human personality is "a living and peopled drama in which the subject 'I' takes part but is neither the sole author, nor director, nor always the main character. Sometimes he or she is not even on stage."[10] This is particularly evident during our dreams when we are flooded with visitors from our inner world, the many faces of our "self." Hillman takes very seriously the Jungian acceptance of psychological complexity; indeed, our personal complexities are considered the persons of our complexes. Jung referred to the person as having "splinter psyches." Hillman speaks of this reality of the soul's multiplicity in terms of a "polytheistic awareness."

Polytheism is a way of speaking about the various archetypal structures or patterns of the soul. A polytheistic viewpoint recognizes the soul's multiplicity. When we are "in soul," we are conscious of our many-sidedness, open to many perspectives, particularly willing to go beyond the perspective of the heroic ego. Soul's multiplicity accounts for the many moods we can pass through. What is needed is to find ways of naming these various experiences. Hillman turns to myth to further this end of understanding soul's polytheism and, when approaching an event, asks, "not *why* or *how*, but rather *what* specifically is being presented and ultimately *who*, which divine figure, is speaking in this style of consciousness, this form of presentation."[11] In short, we can ask what myth are we living at a particular time of our life; what's the myth in this particular mess?

We must keep in mind that when we speak of psychological polytheism, we are speaking of an attitude toward the soul and not a system of belief. The many gods of the soul are to be imagined, not believed in or taken literally. We must not confuse psychological with theological polytheism, since our concern is primarily with psychology, not theology, or more to the point, the psychology within theology. In this vein, Hillman holds up the Jewish tradition as being polytheistic in attitude while monotheistic in belief. This tradition believes in one God, but in refusing to define God and in leaving its belief uncodified, it allows for the witness of volumes of Jewish commentaries with their multitude of images of this God. In a similar vein, a polytheistic attitude allows for more than one archetypal voice to speak to and through the soul. The psychological monotheism that serves the hero myth leads to fundamentalism, which is a death-dealing blow to the soul. The voice of the hero is one voice, but not the only one to be cultivated.

Myth, then, holds a central role in the study of archetypal psychology, serving as its primary rhetoric. We can say mythology is the psychology of antiquity; the logos or speech of myth is the logos or speech of psyche. The various mythic figures reveal the universal patterns that govern the psyche. The gods and goddesses of Greek mythology can serve as metaphors for different modes of experience, and various ways of being in the world. Hillman calls them "cosmic perspectives in which the soul participates."[12] So, we can speak of being in an Apollonian or Dionysian mode or mood, of having an experience that links us with the world and experience of Demeter or Artemis. These mythic figures serve as metaphorical expressions of distinct modes of consciousness. We look to the images of their stories for a deeper understanding of the gestalt or pattern that captures a particular way of being in the world.

An earlier instance of how these archetypal myths were understood to influence our lives can be found in the connection made between mythology and various rhetorical styles during the Renaissance. During that highly imaginative period when the classical figures of the Greek divinities were being rediscovered, rhetoric's different styles of expression were imagined as embodiments of certain gods and goddesses. An argumentative style was linked with Ares, a sensuous style with Aphrodite, an attraction to the wisdom of tradition with Saturn. This approach was the forerunner to delineating the varying experiences of the soul. "The soul's inherent multiplicity demands a theological fantasy of equal differentiation," says Hillman.[13]

Now, if it is possible to apply these mythic figures to ways of being in soul, let us go a further step. If soul is constituted of images, can we speak of images as participating in this same variety of perspectives? Can we speak of an image as functioning in the manner of Aphrodite or Ares, as interacting in our consciousness in a way reminiscent of Apollo or Hermes? This is the move I would like to suggest in relation to the biblical and other preaching images. Furthermore, just as the soul can participate now in one perspective, now in another, so too a biblical image can function now in one mode, now in another, depending on the context and manner in which it is crafted and related to the particular context in which we are preaching.

One may ask: Why turn to these mythic figures for assistance in our work of preaching? What does Greek mythology have to say to our attempt to wrestle with the sacred writings rooted most often in an Hebraic consciousness? I would propose that just as the great contribution of the Hebraic mind was to delineate the first and subsequent stirrings of the revelation of the God revealed in the experience of Israel and then most fully in Jesus of Nazareth and to provide in the books of the Bible an imaginal map of the reality of covenant with this God, so the contribution of Greek mythology was to offer one useful delineation of the various aspects of the human psyche through its figures of the gods and goddesses, charting the territory of the soul and naming its various ways of being in the world. It is one of Hillman's contributions to explicitly link these ancient images with the study of soul and to locate soul's speech in the workings of imagination. I would like to extend this further by using these figures to imagine how the images we offer in our preaching might be understood to function in the consciousness of those before us.

Archetypal psychology draws us to attend to the images of our lives, both in our dreams and in our world. Such images, visual or oral, can have a dramatic impact on our being. Part of this task involves the need to understand the different mythic patterns which characterize how images can "work" in us. Hillman has said that this is a major task now confronting psychology: "the differentiation of the imaginal, discovering its laws, its configurations and moods of discourse, its psychological necessities."[14]

In the coming chapters, we will offer several ways of differentiating the imaginal, of naming some of its configurations and moods of discourse in order to understand the various ways in which a biblical image can enter into the consciousness of a community and interact and influence its vision of life. Before doing this, however, we will consider some general directives found in Hillman's work that facilitate what I call "imaginal preaching."

Imaginal Preaching and Soul-Making: Some General Directives

Imaginal preaching takes seriously Jung's statement that concepts are coined and negotiable, but images are life. If we wish to sustain life in the world, one way is to cultivate the images that will give life. Hillman speaks of a primary principle: "that the thought of the heart is the thought of images, that the heart is the seat of imagination, that imagination is the authentic voice of the heart, so that if we speak from the heart we must speak imaginatively."[15] In order to speak imaginatively, several suggestions can be taken from Hillman's work and taken to heart by preachers.

First of all, *stick to the image*. This is a repeated injunction in Hillman's writings. For Hillman, this involves a refusal to translate an image into a set meaning. An image must not be reduced to an allegory, nor even treated as a symbol that points beyond itself. Its depth is to be found in its very being and that being is inexhaustible and bottomless. Hillman fears that the image will be lost in favor of a concept. He believes that this is already the case with symbols. The traditional

Jungian understanding of a symbol as "the best possible formulation of a relatively unknown thing" has yielded to set meanings. Symbols have become stand-ins for concepts. The precision of the image has given way to the universal quality of the symbol. Hillman's call to "stick to the image" hopes to counteract the tendency to either conceptualize or generalize what is precise in its actual presentation.

"Stick to the image" means to consider all the details and the particular context and mood of an image. We can think of this as befriending the image. Allow the image to speak in its own voice. Watch its behavior. Try to understand it on its own terms rather than rushing in with a pre-conceived understanding. Hillman's opposition to interpretation is due to the tendency to impose a single meaning on an event, image, story, or any imaginal reality. To speak of a good interpretation as one that "clicks" does not satisfy him because it implies a "this and only this" type of correspondence; rather, a good interpretation is one that "stains, ferments, illumines, wounds."

Quite often our tendency when we approach scripture can be to read it hastily because we "know" it. We immediately move to what it is "about." There can be a reflex to reduce the story, parable, or image to a succinct, abstract formulation, a single interpretation. The parable of the prodigal son is *about* forgiveness. The story of Jesus and Zacchaeus is *about* the seeking and saving of one who was lost. Hillman invites us to attend to the image in its precise formulation, trying to see, hear, feel and even smell it, so that something new may come to awareness.

Some examples may be helpful. Walter Vogels, professor of scripture at St. Paul's University in Ottawa, speaks of having given a group the story of Zacchaeus (Lk 19:1-10) to read.[16] After they went over it several times, he asked, "Why did Zacchaeus climb the tree?" Most responded, "To see Jesus." Not exactly. This is not part of the imaginal reality of the story. The text says that he climbed the sycamore "to see what kind of man Jesus was" (v. 3). This detail changes the precise image of the text; it gives a different feel to our initial introduction to Zacchaeus. Each detail is part of the mood and context that the text creates. Each detail deserves attention.

A second example. I can remember working on the text which includes the story of the good Samaritan (Lk 10:25-37). In the course of trying to attend to the text in all its precision, researching some recent commentaries, and some helpful "seeing" in my imagination, I became aware of that pivotal moment in the parable which hinges on a slight movement of the body. The priest and Levite looked and passed by on the other side; the Samaritan looked and "approached" him. It all hinged on that simple movement, a pivotal turn toward the other. This kind of detail is what makes the tale memorable. It awakens and invites play. How did he approach? Did he go by, then hesitate before moving toward, or move immediately toward the body lying on the road, or...? That simple act of "approaching" the other became the single image that fired my imagination and drew me into the story in a fresh way.

Stick to the image. Allow it to work its way into your imagination. Let it speak to you about itself in its own words. Hillman reminds us that images are "powers with claims." He says that they are our "keepers" and we are theirs, "necessary angels" waiting for a response.[17] To stick to the image can initiate a process that is ongoing because an image is bottomless. But an initial commitment must be made. "We can not get to the soul of the image without love for the image."[18] Conversely, love is to be found in the depths of the image, calling to us. This takes us into the area of how we might imagine our interaction with an image. In the next chapter, the myth of Eros and Psyche will be considered for its relevance to this process.

Secondly, *twist the image*. This second directive can, but does not necessarily need to, follow the first. It can function on its own as a distinct way of engaging an image or story. The metaphor of twisting is one of Hillman's efforts to protect the inherent multiplicity of meaning that is to be found in the image or story. Twisting is another way of *playing* with the image. But what about being true to the story? "To be true to the story doesn't mean not to twist it. It means don't forget to tell the story. But not always in the same way, with the same meaning; that's just fundamentalism."[19] The story needs to be retold but it also needs to be twisted; this is what the Jewish tradition did so effectively in its midrash. It retold the story with a twist that gave it new life.

If three people were encouraged to tell the story of the good Samaritan, it might be similar but certainly not identical. Each might present it from a different angle of vision. Each could work with the characters differently. Perhaps a more sympathetic Levite in one, or a gruff Samaritan in another. Perhaps one or the other scene would be from the perspective of a minor character, for instance, the innkeeper to whom the Samaritan takes the wounded man. Encouraging people to twist the story by being creative with the characters or with the angle from which a scene is described can open it up in unexpected ways.

I can remember an exercise that the storyteller Robert Bela Wilhelm had participants try during a week's workshop in storytelling that provided a way to twist a tale. He asked us to choose a favorite story from the scriptures; then, after we had told that in a small group, he asked us to go back and think about telling it from the perspective of one of the objects in the story. I had chosen to tell the story of David's receiving word about the death of his son Absalom. In the retelling I imagined the scene of David pacing up and down in the courtyard of the palace, awaiting word of what had happened to Absalom. This time I imagined myself as a set of steps that led up to his private quarters. I became these steps, with a view of the pacing king, but also gifted with its own memories. I recalled how it used to feel to have the feet of the king's children—Absalom, Tamar, and Amnon—fall upon me as they raced up to greet their father, and of the weight of the king himself at different times of his life, times of success and failure. But all this dwindled to a shadow memory when word finally came to the king and I felt the weight not only of his body but of his heart as he pulled himself up each of my steps. Then, at the top, his grief-stricken cry that silenced the world, "Absalom, my son, my son, Absalom. If only I had died instead of you, Absalom, my son, my son."

This exercise took the story and twisted it. That story made David and his grief real to me and my listeners in a way that might not have occurred without that twist of seeing, hearing, feeling the event from the perspective of a stairway, given a memory and an ability to tell the tale. Hillman makes a provocative comment when he says that to give a story a new twist, you have to be in touch with your own pathology because that's where the twist comes from. I think this has to do with image's power to speak to one's *pathos*, to touch the depths of one's emotion and suffering, and to evoke a response from that level. It involves a response from the level of one's own need, one's deepest feeling, and one's own wounds.

Thirdly, *craft the image*. This last directive can be seen as a logical step after the first two. After sticking with the image in all its precise details as it is given to us in a biblical text and/or after engaging in the playful activity of twisting the image, one attempts to craft the result. When dealing with the imaginal that comes in dreams or fantasy, Hillman suggests a number of ways an image can be crafted: painting, sculpting, drawing or some other physically expressive form. And such attempts at crafting in other media may be helpful for preachers, provided they put on "hold" any perfectionistic tendency to create a work of "art."

At some point, the crafting, molding, and shaping of the image will turn to the medium of words. We are invited to take part in an act of *poesis*, a making or shaping of an imaginal reality through carefully chosen words. Hillman reminds us of the power of this medium when he says, "without the inherence of soul in words, speech would not move us, words would not provide forms for carrying our lives and giving sense to our deaths."[20]

To craft the image with words means to enter into an active engagement with the image. One of Hillman's suggestions is to avoid approaching an image solely as a picture because that makes the experience too optical, in addition to intellectual and distant. Instead, he proposes that the image be imagined as a scene, as something that I can get into, and as a mood, as something that gets into me. This is reminiscent of the advice to preachers not to preach *on* the scriptures but *from* and *through* them. Such an invitation allows all our senses to engage with the image. How does it look, smell, taste, feel, sound? Experiment with the words so the image is as fully present as possible. An image, well crafted, can draw others into its world and encourage their own crafting.

The preacher's responsible crafting of the images preserved in the biblical texts is one way to overturn the loss of soul found even in the world of religion. Through crafted images sown into the consciousness of a community, soul can be awakened, cultivated, and engaged. While the dominant lens here is psychological, a theological awareness is never entirely distant, for behind all that is said is the presence of that divine force which is Love incarnate. As already noted, these images do not deserve to be treated merely as decorative coverings for abstract formulations of truth, but can be approached as living presences that mediate an encounter with Mystery. We are called to continue the process that is part of the Judaeo-Christian tradition in which God impressed his image most perfectly on one like us and embodied that image in flesh. In the intervening centuries, this image of the invisible God has impressed itself on the senses, hearts, and minds of men and women who have been transformed by it. We have now been entrusted with the craftings of the divine image found in the scriptures. Now our own skill at crafting images must come into play.

For this crafting to occur, preachers must first love the images that have been cared for over the centuries. From this relationship, new life will come for the preacher and, through the preacher, for the community. Hillman has stated that love abides in the image, reaching out for soul. Images can hold us; we can lie in their embrace. Hillman invites us to think of image as having a body, a subtle body, and calls us to engage in an erotic approach to the imaginal world. To understand this dynamic more fully, we will turn to the myth of Eros and Psyche and its implications and challenge for the preacher.

3.

Eros and the
Homiletic Process

"Eros is never something we have; it has us."
James Hillman

The Experience of Eros

Hillman's vision of the soul invites us to see all events, actions, and experiences as participations in the mythic world of the gods and goddesses. If we ask, "what god, what archetypal force, is hidden in the homiletic process?" the answer I propose is, "Eros." Eros, the god of love, the principle of connection and relatedness, is at the heart of the homiletic endeavor because preaching's end is to establish, foster, and deepen union with the divine and with others.

The popular image of Eros is the diminutive and overly sentimentalized Cupid, the banalized figure on Valentine cards, rendered cute and huggable by ringlets of curls, a tiny bow, and a quiver of arrows. But the god Eros is a more forceful and foreboding figure, a fact captured in the varying accounts of his origin. One tradition says he is the oldest god, born from Chaos, emerging out of the gaping chasm as its first utterance. Another version says he is a member of the brood of Night, brother of Hypnos (Sleep) and Thanatos (Death). Still another recounts that he is the child of Aphrodite and Ares, forever linked with passionate conflicts and conflicting passions. Our interest in Eros will be limited to the myth of Eros and Psyche, pertinent not only for an understanding of all love relationships but also for offering insight into the awakening and engen-

Eros and Psyche.

dering of the imagination. In fact, these two areas of loving and imagining intertwine when we consider Eros' relevance for the experience of preaching.

Let us begin with the most common experience of Eros. When two people "fall in love," they are said to be under this power. There is a sense of being out of control, of being taken over by a force stronger than reason. The pangs of love are captured in the image of Eros with a torch, singeing the wings of a butterfly, or as a figure shooting or wounding a young girl. And when we speak of being in love, we talk of feeling "on fire," of "burning" with passion, in addition to feeling weakened and wounded. Erotic love is a consuming love, a willing or unwilling self-immolation. Eros is a transcendent force outside of the individual whose entrance into one's world brings both torture and transcendence, pain and joy.

Hillman links this most common experience of Eros with an awakening of psyche or imagination in the lover. He writes that for the lover "the other person has become a mysterious incendiary, some kind of fuse that ignites the imagination concretely, makes the imagination terribly, passionately real, physical, alive, desirable...."[1] Reflection on experience confirms this response. Eros does awaken our soul, our imagination. When we are in love with another, that other is the locus of Eros' presence, stirring our imagination into new life. We cannot stop thinking about the person; we call up memories of moments shared; we daydream about the person in scenarios yet to take place. The imagination is very much activated and energized. Images flow freely. In this way, Eros continually calls to Psyche, awakening her and stirring up the desire for union.

But the meeting place of lovers is not the only sacred space; Eros also makes his way into every place where soul-making is happening, from the counseling room where people come to heal their souls, to the church where they come to save them. How does Eros behave in the sacred precincts of worship? The words of H.G. Baynes offer a possible hint:

> the essential character of Eros is the divine (i.e., creative) shaft which leaps across the guarded frontier of the subject in order to reach the object. The creative shaft is the impregnating phallus, the impressive, fertilizing image, the creative word, the idea which gets home....[2]

When we begin to think of Eros as the "impressive, fertilizing image, the creative word, the idea which gets home," Eros has entered into human communication, the act of speaking, which includes preaching. We find him in a speaking event when we are moved, touched by a speaker's words, when our hearts burn within us. Beneath these clichés lurks divinity. Preaching can qualify as one realm where Eros seeks union with Psyche. Since preaching aims to bind a community in a deeper union with God and each other through the biblical word, and since the role of the imagination is central to this bonding, Eros will be considered as a key figure in our attempt to articulate an archetypal foundation for preaching. This figure speaks not only to the experience of effective preaching but the myth of Eros and Psyche sheds light on the process of preaching preparation. We will begin with a retelling of the myth, then consider its value as a paradigm for awakening the preacher's soul as he or she prepares to preach.

The Myth of Eros and Psyche[3]

Once there was a king and queen who had three daughters. The youngest was named Psyche. She was beautiful beyond words. Those who looked upon her thought she was the goddess Aphrodite incarnate, which did not please the goddess at all. All who gazed upon Psyche were in such awe that the shrines and altars of Aphrodite were neglected. This led the goddess to call upon her son Eros and enlist his help in rectifying such a shameful situation.

Eros was known as a very bad boy who had neither manners nor regard for treating anyone with respect, even the other gods and goddesses. He was always ready to play his cruel tricks. When he responded to his mother's call, Aphrodite commanded him to send his arrow of love into the heart of Psyche so she would be bound to the meanest man alive, one so vile that he was a perfect outcast, having neither wealth, honor, or comeliness. But when Eros gazed upon Psyche, he was so overcome by her beauty that he dropped the arrow he had ready for her on his own foot and became wounded by his own weapon of enchantment.

In the meantime the king was troubled because, though all thought his youngest most beautiful, awe kept them at a distance. No one approached to ask for her hand. Psyche sat at home, lonely, sick in spirit, adored but not loved. So the king went to the oracle of Apollo to seek advice. The oracle told him that his daughter was to be the bride of one whom the very gods feared and that he was to take his daughter in bridal garments and leave her on the top of the mountain until one, fierce, wild and born of the dragon, would come for her.

And so it came to pass that Psyche, dressed in wedding garb, was left at the peak of a high mountain. Her wedding procession had been more that of a funeral, with the songs turning to dirges. After all had left her, darkness surrounded her as she sat trembling, waiting for what would come next. Suddenly a gentle breeze lifted her and carried her off the mountain, laying her in a valley in a bed of flowers. Then Psyche slept. The next day when she awoke, she found herself near a grove of tall trees, by a cool flowing stream, and within sight of a beautiful castle so enchanting that she thought it must belong to one even more powerful than her father.

Gathering her courage, she went up to the house and entered. Passing through the rooms, each more beautiful than the last the more deeply she went into the house, Psyche heard a voice say, "All is thine, Psyche! And we are your servants. Command us and it shall be done as you have said." And so Psyche ate and drank and bathed to the accompaniment of sweet music.

That night Eros came to her and embraced her in the darkness. His voice was soft and gentle, "Dearest Psyche, ask not my name, nor try to look upon my face. Believe in my love and all will be well." Psyche's heart was won. Through the night Eros spoke his love but as daybreak threatened, he kissed her and promised to return with the night. And so the nights passed and the days in like manner. All day Psyche was alone; at night her love would come. As time went on, Psyche began to live for the nights and dread the days. The beautiful house began to feel like a cage. She begged her love to stay but he whispered, "Danger hovers over you and will descend if you discover who I am." Finally she asked if her sisters could come and visit her. Eros tried to prevent this, fearing what would happen. "They bring hate and peril for our love," he warned. But Psyche continued to entreat him and he finally relented.

At first the sisters were overwhelmed by their sister's good fortune, but soon enough, their wonder changed to jealousy and they tricked from Psyche the secret that she had never laid eyes on her beloved, even though she was pregnant with his child. "He is a monster, a beast, a huge serpent" they shouted, "and he will devour you and your unborn child." "What shall I do?" Psyche pleaded. They replied, "This night, after he has fallen asleep, take a lamp to your bed so you can look upon this monster and carry a knife to plunge into his heart." That night Eros came with the darkness. When she believed him to be asleep, Psyche got up from the bed and went over to the table.

Lighting the lamp and picking up the knife, she walked toward the bed. As the light fell over his form, Psyche was stunned; beautiful beyond words was the creature that lay before her. So overwhelmed was she that the knife dropped from her hand. Looking down she saw his bow and quiver and leaning over to draw out one of his arrows, she pricked her finger, immediately becoming inflamed even more deeply with love for her newly seen beloved. Bending over to kiss him, Psyche forgot about the lamp and a drop of oil fell upon his shoulder. Jumping up, Eros looked into the eyes of Psyche and realized all that had happened. "You have ruined our love! Why did you listen to your sisters? Now we must part forever." And off he flew. The castle vanished and Psyche was completely alone in the darkness. As for Eros, he fled to the home of his mother Aphrodite, where she confined him to a room.

At first Psyche attempted to throw herself in the river, so full of anguish and despair was she. But a friendly river god gently returned her to the shore. Psyche then came upon the god Pan who encouraged her to seek out her love. In the meantime

Aphrodite had found out what had happened, how her own son
had disobeyed her, and was now reaping the fruits of his wrong-
headed independence. In a rage, the goddess sent out word that
the young girl was to be given over to her, and heaven help anyone who would come to her aid. Eventually Psyche heard of this
and, having nowhere else to go, came to the castle of Aphrodite.

When she entered, she was seized by the hair and dragged before
the goddess. "Now you will learn what it means to rival
Aphrodite," shrieked the goddess. Thus began what is known as
the great trials of Psyche. First, Psyche was brought into a room
before a mountain of tiny seeds—wheat, peas, beans, barley—
and Aphrodite demanded that each kind be put into a separate
pile, and that this be done by evening. And off the goddess went
to a wedding feast, beautifully coiffed and as charming as could
be, looking forward to how she would chastise Psyche on her
return.

Psyche stood before the mound of seeds in a state of despair. She
could not lift a finger, so hopeless did she feel. But an ant happened to be going by and he looked at Psyche and looked at the
mountain, then he did it once again. Taking pity, the ant called out
his troop and one by one the seeds were separated and sorted, collected into the appropriate piles. Then they disappeared. When
Aphrodite returned, she was astonished. "This is not your doing,
you wench, nor the work of your hands, but the work of him
whose heart you won to your own hurt, and his hurt too."

The next day Psyche was sent to retrieve some of the golden
fleece from a flock of sheep. "They are ferocious and their bite is
venomous, my dear. But do what you can, before the sun sets,"
said Aphrodite as she sent off the young girl. Going to the top of a
hill, Psyche once again thought of casting herself into the river.
But from the riverbed, a green reed cried out and said, "Psyche,
do not cast yourself into the water, but wait. These sheep are now
playing under the heat of the sun. Soon the sun will tire them and
they will be still; then they will cease standing and take their
afternoon rest. At that time, you can gather their fleece from the

briars of the nearby grove where they have wandered." And so it happened. Psyche was able to gather a whole lapful of golden wool. When Psyche gave over the golden fleece to Aphrodite, the goddess was enraged and again said, "This is not your work but the work of another, just as the last."

"But here," Aphrodite continued, "I have another task for you. And it will take you to a place where there is no one to help. Look up at that mountain rising into the clouds before you and see the black stream which flows in cataracts from the crest. Take this crystal jar and fill it with this water. But do be careful of the dragons that guard it." When Psyche finally came near to the base of the mountain and looked up to see its peak disappear into the clouds, she sat down in despair. But, once again, help was not absent. The eagle of Zeus, who once had been aided by Eros, suddenly swept down and seized the crystal urn from her hand. Flying between the dragons, it dipped down and for a moment was lost in the cataracts. Immediately it was seen again, returning to Psyche with the crystal vase filled with water from the Stygian springs. Psyche thanked the eagle and took it back to the goddess of love. But, again, she found no diminishment of Aphrodite's disdain, nor sign of a reprieve.

Then, the goddess ordered Psyche to go down to the underworld and bring back in a box some of the beauty of Persephone. Yet again Psyche was on the edge of despair, this time atop a tower, ready to cast herself off. Who had gone to the nether world and ever returned? Still, she thought that by throwing herself off, she would at least reach the region of Hades where Persephone lived. However, the tower itself began to speak to her and tell her about another way. The tower advised Psyche, instructing her how to avoid the pitfalls of getting to and from Hades. All the tower could give was advice; Psyche had to carry out the advice as she went along. In the end she trusted the tower and did all that she had been told, which included taking a coin to pay the boatman Charon to buy passage across the river Styx, resisting the call for help of a man floating in the river as she was crossing, avoiding the lame driver who asked assistance with his lame animal, and, finally, paying no attention to the pleas coming from the three women weaving, cutting, and stitching at the roadside.

Psyche successfully reached Hades and asked Persephone for some of her beauty to take back in a box to Aphrodite. On the way back, however, Psyche let her curiosity once more win out and looked into the box Persephone had given. This caused her to fall into a deadly sleep. In the meantime, Eros had learned what his mother was up to. Escaping through a window, he found Psyche and by his kisses roused her. Professing his love, he sent her on to his mother while he flew up to the house of Zeus. There he professed his love for Psyche and asked that the father-god allow this marriage and that Zeus transform Psyche into an immortal. And so Zeus decreed, thinking it was time for this spoiled child of Olympus to settle down. And all came to the wedding, even Aphrodite who led the dance.

Thus, in the company of all the gods and goddesses, Eros and Psyche were wed and began to live life in the light of Olympus. And this is how Psyche, once lovely and alone, came to dwell in the company of all the gods and goddesses. And Eros, that mischievous, troublesome child, grew through what he suffered and what was suffered for him. In time their child was born, and she was called Joy (Pleasure).

The Myth and the Awakening of the Imagination

There have been several psychological interpretations of this myth, most notably those found in works by Erich Neumann and Marie Louise Von Franz, the former using it as a model of concerns of feminine psychology and the latter as a model of issues for masculine psychology.[4] But I have found James Hillman's treatment the most helpful for our purposes since he discusses it as a myth of psychological creativity, referring to the process whereby the archetypal force Eros awakens and engenders the psyche or imagination.[5] Hillman does not limit this event to the therapist's office, though it certainly occurs there in the transference phenomenon, but he places its re-enactment out in the world whenever and wherever a connection occurs that means something to the soul. When John falls for Mary, when Carole is moved to tears by a charismatic speaker, when a preacher stirs the hearts of his or her listeners—in all these, Eros awakens Psyche.

We experience Eros when our imagination is stirred to feel a connection with an "other," whether that other is a person, an object, or a text. Eros can be found in the *image* of the "other" which, in turn, awakens our imagining ability. "The lover is bewitched and obsessed by the image of the other," writes Aldo Carotenuto, a Jungian analyst, adding that love is "a generator of images."[6] The myth of Eros and Psyche captures the necessary process by which soul is awakened and transformed into a life-giving capacity in relationship with all the archetypal powers. For this to happen, Eros has to appear and Psyche has to love and lose him, and then undergo the trials. Only after this does Psyche bring forth life and enter into communion with the other gods and goddesses. Before considering the importance of this entire process for the preacher, here is an example of Eros awakening the imagination of another.

When I first began to investigate this myth and its implications for preaching as a creative process, I happened to see the British film, *DreamChild*. In its fictional exploration of the relationship between Charles Dodgson, better known to the world as Lewis Carroll, and Alice Liddell, the young girl who inspired the *Alice* stories, I found a most powerful re-enactment of the Eros-Psyche myth. I want to emphasize the movie is fictional and it is open to other interpretations, but for me the most satisfying hermeneutic was provided by looking through the lens of this ancient myth.

The movie focuses on an event in the later life of Alice Liddell, when she is now the eighty year old Mrs. Hargreaves, who comes to New York City to take part in a centennial celebration of Carroll's birth at Columbia University. In the course of this event, Mrs. Hargreaves' soul becomes the ground for suffering that eventually results in an inner transformation. Her soul is awakened and loved into being by Eros, just as Carroll's soul was similarly awakened decades ago. The movie can be understood as a prolonged meditation on the truthfulness of the Eros and Psyche myth: Eros will seek out Psyche in the other and Psyche will strive to attain union with Eros. We find this played out in the relationship of the two principals and also, in a more predictable way, in the love that springs up between the two secondary characters, Jack, a New York reporter, and Lucy, the young companion of Mrs. Hargreaves.

Alice Liddell Hargreaves is presented as a conflicted and frightened elderly woman, wearing a no-nonsense, Victorian face to the world and an exhausted, anxious face to her mirror. When reporters besiege her with questions and foolish remarks as soon as she arrives in New York, she is firm in rebuking their bad manners, going on to advise the children of the United States to say their prayers, be respectful of their elders, and read with sufficient light on, "though not so much as to cast away all the shadows." With her young companion Lucy, she is often harsh and insensitive, even refusing a simple request to watch dancing couples the last night at sea. But we soon discover that Mrs. Hargreaves is being tormented by hallucinations, memories, and nightmares that come unbidden. "He's coming for me," she tells Lucy. "Mr. Dodgson is coming for me." Dodgson is long dead, but lives in Alice's past memories of her old tutor and in the sudden appearances both he and his literary creations make into Mrs. Hargreaves' life. On one occasion, the March Hare and Mad Hatter are having tea in Mrs. Hargreave's sitting room and, upon seeing the elderly woman, dismiss her as ugly and old; at another time, the Caterpillar calls her "old baggage." Yet, as strange as it sounds, in these images, Eros is pursuing Psyche right up to the end.

In flashbacks we see that the myth of Eros and Psyche was first lived out in her childhood, when the middle-aged mathematics tutor, Mr. Dodgson, was utterly smitten by young Alice. Scenes of her relationship with her stuttering, infatuated teacher are marked by a child's ability to be both loving and cruel. No matter how he is treated, it is clearly seen that *her image* has bewitched him. Besides Dodgson's delight in photographing her again and again and dedicating his works to her, there is an unsettling scene when the whole family is out for a Sunday boat ride, and Dodgson is staring so intently at the young Alice that she splashes water on him, as if to cool him down. Eros first abides in the image of this child, awakening Dodgson's soul and transforming him into Lewis Carroll. His imagination gave us the *Alice* books and the wonderful poems, due to the power of Eros residing in this child.

The beauty of the film is that it completes the circle by showing Eros coming to awaken Mrs. Hargreaves some seventy years later. On the eve of the centenary, in a relaxed moment, she confesses to Lucy and Jack that "I have always been afraid of that emotion [love], though I can recognize it in others." But Eros will not be stopped and the suffering that Mrs. Hargreaves undergoes finally moves her to a new place, passing through Hades to a more calm, if not Olympian, haven. In the sacred hall where the centennial liturgy is celebrated, Alice Liddell Hargreaves finally knows a freedom that allows her to depart from her scripted remarks to publicly acknowledge that long ago she did not recognize the love of Dodgson for the gift that it was, but now, at last, she can say, "Thank you, Mr. Dodgson. Thank you."

DreamChild shows the viewer a very different love story in which Eros seeks Psyche and Psyche needs Eros. It shows that this mythic re-enactment occurs not only between people but between an individual and the imaginal world of memory, dream, and literary creation. In this chapter I would propose that something similar can, indeed *should*, happen in the interaction between the preacher and the biblical text. Eros present in the image of the biblical text seeks to awaken Psyche, the imagining capacity, of the preacher. And the sermon that results, centered in biblical imagery, may act, in turn, as Eros to the Psyche of the gathered community, awakening and engendering it.

Eros in image awakens imagination. In this way, the myth can function both as an expression of the archetypal power that calls to our souls from the images of the scriptural and liturgical texts, but also as an articulation of the process the preacher must undergo in the homiletic engagement with these texts, for the text as Eros calls the preacher to undergo the trials that will lead to deep union, new life, and communion with other archetypal forces. Let us attend once more to the movement of the myth and its relationship to the preaching task.

The Myth and Imaginal Preaching

The Eros-Psyche myth offers preachers a unique way to view their interaction with the scriptures in preparing to preach. When we imagine the biblical images as the home of Eros, we know that love isn't some independent force outside of and apart from the images, but it is right inside them, ready to break into fire and inflame us. Only when our soul has come into union with Eros in the biblical text can new life and new communion come about. For this reason we will look more closely at the movement of the myth: from Psyche as isolated and abandoned young woman, to Psyche as bride to Eros, mother of Joy (Pleasure) and companion of the gods and goddesses.

The myth can be divided into four segments: 1) the transition from the lonely daughter of the king to her first union with Eros in the dark; 2) the night of crisis; 3) the four trials; and 4) the final union in the immortal realm. Each of these parts offers insight into the process of preaching preparation. Preacher and text come from two different worlds. To *dwell with* a text, to enter into communion with it, is crucial to preaching in a manner that will touch the hearts of others. It is not an automatic process. Furthermore, the understanding of this myth as an expression of a true love relationship reminds us that two subjectivities are also involved in our task, the "I" of the preacher and the "thou" of the text.

1) Like Psyche in the beginning of the story, the soul of the preacher can be seen to exist in a solitary state as one begins to prepare to preach on a particular text. The myth's Psyche is first presented as one who is admired but untouched. She is called the "new Aphrodite" by those who look on her. Neumann notes that this is true because mythically she will show a new way to love, not by dominating Eros as the goddess Aphrodite does, but by seeking, suffering, and striving for union. So, too, the soul of the preacher is called to witness to a new way of loving the text, not dominating or manipulating it to say what he or she wishes, but by a willingness to undergo whatever task is necessary for a true union to result.

It is Eros who first gazes upon Psyche and loves her, setting in motion what must happen for them to meet. And it is the living word of God that first comes for us, calls us into communion, leads us apart. The myth relates that the more deeply Psyche entered into the home of Eros, the more beautiful it became, which corresponds to the immersion called for in the exhortation to dwell in the text.

The first union with Eros is, significantly, "in the dark." He only comes at night. This has been compared to the infatuation phase of any loving relationship, that period of living in a fool's paradise, of total bliss. But this stage is not meant to last. This is comparable to a first naive understanding of the text, a play-it-as-it-lays approach, being satisfied with a first reading's superficial awareness of the scripture. To embrace the text this superficial way is to live with it in the dark. In the story, the sisters serve the function of waking Psyche to the fact that she lives in a lovely prison, one of her own choice. In our own experience, contemporary biblical scholarship with its various critical approaches provides multiple voices that call us out of the dark, to look at what is before us.

2) The second phase begins when Psyche makes the decision to look upon Eros, to take a light and gaze upon him, and to carry the knife to dispatch him if he should prove to be a monster. Similarly, the preacher must approach the text to gaze upon it, "looking with understanding." The late Roman Catholic theologian Romano Guardini talked about such looking when he wrote that "the condition of all valid seeing and hearing, upon every plane of consciousness, lies not in a sharpening of the senses, but in a particular attitude of the whole personality: in a self-forgetting attentiveness, a profound concentration, a self-merging which operates a real communion between the seer and the seen—in a word, in contemplation."[7] Preachers must choose to look at what is before them.

3) Psyche's desire to see Eros awakens him and necessitates her undergoing the four trials to reach a union with Eros in the light. Similarly, the decision to look upon the text moves the preacher toward a new relationship with it. The trials are the heart of the myth; therefore, we will consider each trial separately, for they are also at the heart of an imaginal approach to preaching. By undergoing these trials, the first union ends and a new one can begin.

The first trial is the ordering of the seeds. When one gazes upon a text, attentive to the possibility for a "real communion," one attends to what is there, whether we understand this as a "self-forgetting attentive-ness" which centers on the attitude of the preacher or as a call to "stick to the image" which focuses immediately on the imaginal quality of the text. Just as Psyche is confronted with a state of chaos, thousands of seeds of different kinds that need to be sorted and ordered, so too the preacher who begins to attend to a text can become lost in a world of images that need to be collected and sorted.

When one first attends to the images found in a text, a particular image may first capture one's attention, but in time, usually another will come to the fore; then perhaps something comes to mind from the world in front of the text, from something in today's paper or nightly news or a scene from a movie. Gather the images that come, both those in the text, and those the text attracts. Image begets image. Eventually, you will need to begin to sort and order them. This can be done in a number of ways—for instance, by allowing certain images to be dominant and subordinating others to them, or by choosing one dominant image and relating others to it in a sequence determined by the text or linked by a free association. This is not the time for editing or censoring what is coming forth. Gather, sort and order the seeds with potential for new life—this is the first task.

A final observation on this first trial. In her commentary on this myth, Van Franz draws our attention to the role of the ants as being linked with the work of the unconscious.[8] The unconscious is connected with both chaos and order. When we experience the chaos of the unconscious, if we wait long enough, order—like the ants—will also come forth from the unconscious. In the process of collecting images, the unconscious works within us, sending up images linked directly and indirectly with the text. We do not do this alone. This is emphasized in the tale when Aphrodite says to Psyche, after she has completed this task, "This is not just your doing, but the doing of another, the one whose heart you won...." The myth itself reminds us that every part of this enterprise of awakening the imagination is ultimately attributed to Eros, the archetypal force that relates and connects.

As an instance of the task represented by the first trial, we might consider the gospel reading assigned in the Roman Catholic lectionary for the feast of the birth of St. John the Baptist on June 24 (Lk 1:57-66.80). First we gather the images of the text: a baby laid into the arms of its elderly mother, the friends and family joyfully gathered for a celebration on the day the child is to be named and circumcised, the hush that falls when the mother says, "His name is John" (everyone had already been calling him Zechariah as they were passing him around), the tension as they gently point out "but none of your relatives has this name"; then, the turn toward Zechariah, struck mute since that day nine months ago in the temple, Zechariah's response of wild gesturing, until someone hands him a tablet and he scrawls in large letters, "HIS NAME IS JOHN!!!" Finally, the tongue is loosened and there is a flood of words, not in explanation but in praise. Fear, dismay, wonder descend with the evening sun on the little town. A final image as epilogue: a child growing up and living in the desert, in solitude.

The first move is to gather and sort the images. As you hear the text, what do you see? Allow your imagination to work with the images. Stick to what is given, but allow yourself to engage all your senses. See the look on Elizabeth's face as the child is placed in her arms for the first time and also the expression on her face as she says, "His name is John." And again, when the neighbors, friends and even family turn from her, dismissing her, toward Zechariah, what does her face register? Are there other images that come to you from your own experience that help you to enter this text—memories of family parties, the feel of the tension that can suddenly occur at a family gathering when someone goes against the "rules" of the family. First, immerse yourself in the world of the text and its images. Then, allow the text to pull in images from life. Gather, collect, sort.

The second trial sends Psyche out to gather the golden wool from the ferocious sheep. Once again, near despair, Psyche contemplates suicide, but a river reed offers advice: "Wait until the sun tires them and they rest." Like sheep, images can be resistant to being tamed, but the role of the sun here points us toward the light of reflective consciousness. Time spent pondering and meditating on an image will allow the ideas it contains to surface, bearing the thought it carries. One must allow time for the light of reflection to shine down and through the images that have been gathered.

At this second stage we pause to think about what these images say, what thought they contain, and to investigate what others have to say about a text, making use of all the biblical scholarship that has resulted from the various methodologies and perspectives presently in use. Now we turn to the studies of biblical historical criticism, literary and rhetorical criticism, structuralism, and the various perspectives (feminist, liberation theology, etc.) that have made important contributions to our understanding of the scriptures' meaning.

The sequence is important. Before moving to the biblical commentaries, allow time with the images first. The traditional approach to preaching a text looked immediately for the ideas it contained or the doctrines the text could be used to support. In this way, the imaginal quality of a text was lost. The tendency was to move away quickly from the text's literary and aesthetic characteristics, discarding them as so much decoration, and arrive at the text's inner meaning, usually reduced to abstract, conceptual formulations. But, remember, Psyche doesn't have to kill the sheep to gather the golden wool; she waits for the sun to quiet them. Without the sheep, there would be no wool; they are its carriers. Similarly, though we move from the colorful world of experience to the thought contained, we do not abandon the former. The images carry the thought.

Study and reflection on this text from Luke[9] brought me the following understanding of its meaning: a) This segment is the second diptych of Luke's Prologue, itself a literary device that contains many Lukan themes found throughout the Gospel/Acts; here the birth of John is presented as a parallel to the birth of Jesus, just as both have annunciation accounts. The Prologue functions to set forth and highlight the identity of Jesus, and proposes that John is to be seen in relation to this end. b) In this particular excerpt, God has overcome the restrictions of old age and barrenness and directly intervened in the birth of this child. It is an event of wonder. c) A new age is dawning, captured in the birth and naming of this child; a new name is given first by his mother, then confirmed by his father. d) The father's tongue is loosed at the birth of the child, a liberation that breaks forth into praise. In addition, I find particularly intriguing the father's being silenced before and until the son is born.

The third trial sends Psyche with a crystal vase to get some of the gushing black water, symbol of death and rebirth, flowing in cataracts from a mountain crest guarded by two dragons. Psyche stands there, waiting for help. The eagle of Zeus achieves this impossible goal. The eagle has been spoken of as the symbol of that intuitive spirit that comes from the unconscious. Von Franz writes:

> Great creation comes always from the depths; if we can keep in contact with the depths of our psyche, we will have the possibility of giving form to that which wants to be expressed through us.[10]

This trial speaks to the need in preaching preparation for help from beyond, that intuitive flight that comes as a gift and brings the life-giving water in a contained vessel. Up to this time, we have gathered images and waited for their thought to come forth. But it is possible for this to go on forever. Such is the case with preaching that has many stories, images, thoughts, but no sense of cohesion. Containment is needed, something that unifies and yet allows for fluidity. We are concerned here with structure but also with that nucleus that is the heart of any preaching endeavor. One can think of this in different ways, as a controlling image, a dominant idea, or a narrative flow that allows image and thought to move with purpose.

The vase speaks of limits and containment. Only a certain amount can be held; that is all that is needed. Similarly, all the images gathered and all the ideas flowing from them will not be employed, only enough to be contained in an appropriate vessel. To return to the Lukan text for a moment, at some point a simple statement "came" to me: "The voice of the priest must be silenced until the prophet is born; then it bursts forth in praise." That served as the heart of the homily that was given.

In the fourth trial Psyche must go to the underworld to bring back a box of beauty from Persephone. This trial reveals two things of importance. Beauty can be absent from the earth. Our age has done much to repress beauty, not only from the earth, but also from language. Secondly, there comes a time in preparation when the soul must come into its own, taking on responsibility for achieving union with Eros present in the image. To the gathering of images, the recollection of ideas, and the imposition of a structure to contain a limited but sufficient amount of life-giving water, is added the necessity of beauty.

We also find in this final trial a word of caution: the soul can become bewitched by beauty. Psyche's trance can be seen as imagination's capacity to become so absorbed by beauty that it does not reach those for whom it is given. I have seen some beginning preachers become so entranced by the crafted beauty of their texts that they become lifeless in the moment of communicating their message. Striving to give each word as it is written, they become so absorbed in their text and the beauty of it that communication is blocked and the experience of its beauty is limited to its author and never really arrives at its proper destination, the community.

This final trial that precedes union with Eros involves the soul's act of bringing beauty back to the world; it is an issue of aesthetics, from the Greek *aesthesis*, which refers to both the act of perceiving and the act of feeling. One wants the listeners to perceive and feel the beauty of the image, to be touched by it. When others are touched by a sermon, soul is awakened, inflamed. Indeed, the word sermon is rooted in the Indo-European *ser* which means to attach, to join one thing to another. The preaching hopes to join divinity and humanity, preacher and people, through the crafted beauty of the imaginal language.

The final stage of the story shows Psyche in union with Eros, this time not in darkness but in the full light of day where all the gods and goddesses dwell. This reunion corresponds to the new relationship between the imagination of the preacher and the biblical text. Such a reunion, which is the result of the trials that Psyche has undergone, sets the stage for the birth of Joy. I find it interesting that the name of the child in the myth is sometimes rendered Joy, sometimes Pleasure. The Brazilian philosopher Rubem Alves speaks of the difference between these two experiences.[11] He says that pleasure is something that exists only in the present and can be seen as the discharge of dammed energy, the prototype being the orgasm. When pleasure is achieved, one enters a state of rest and becomes desireless. Joy, however, while it involves the present, also embraces the past, allowing it to become present. Alves says "joy is not discharge. It is reunion." Even when the experience is past, one can bring it back in memory and know joy. Such a distinction can be applied to the two different experiences we can have of Eros. While Pleasure may be the child of Eros and Psyche in the experience of falling in love and expressing that love physically, Joy seems the appropriate name for the experience of Eros as a fertilizing image, the impregnating word that links past with present. The homily uses the words and images of the past to address the present and make it fruitful.

The preaching that results from viewing the preparation process as a reliving of the Eros-Psyche myth is meant to honor the images of the text and facilitate their interaction with the lives of listeners. It is meant to mediate an encounter with mystery. Here is the opening of one such effort on the feast of St. John the Baptist's birth.

The Silence of the Priest, the Sound of the Prophet

From the barren couple came a song-filled son.
From the priestly pair, the watchman of the dawn.
Elizabeth's eyes lit up the room
    when his mouth reached for her breasts,
    no longer shrivelled but filled with milk.

And Zechariah's tongue found new freedom,
   once the wildly gesturing hands
   settled for a pen's limits
   and scrawled, "John! His Name is John!"
And neighbors stepped back,
   stunned at the torrent of praise that broke forth,
   sunning the room.

We are a priestly people
And we are a people with priests.
And we sometimes fail as both.
And innocent life does not come to birth,
   or worse yet, once born, is damaged and abused.

We can presume much—
   having a corner on wisdom, integrity,
   righteousness, the truth.
And so, the story of Zechariah might be instructive.
Zechariah the priest reminds us that at times
   the voice of the priest needs to know silence
      to find faith again
      to allow God to work in new ways
      to bring the voice of the prophet to life.

Otherwise,
   the world will not know the new age:
      the horn of salvation that *is* raised
         up in our day
      and the dawning from on high that this day
         visits us.
And we, as a priestly people and a people of priests,
   will not know the new freedom
   that comes only when a prophetic voice is born,
      freeing us for praise and holiness of life,
         in our time and in time to come.

One final comment is made not only as a conclusion to this chapter but as a link to the remainder of this work. Eros weds Psyche in the presence of all the gods and goddesses. He has won immortality for her and is her access into communion with all the divinities of Olympus. When Jung wrote of Eros, he called him "a kosmogonos, a creator and father-mother of all higher consciousness."[12] For Jung, "higher consciousness" was the realm of the collective unconscious, the world of the archetypes, the forces that served as the basic, universal patterns of human existence. Through Eros the soul comes into contact with the variety of archetypal worlds that the gods and goddesses represent. Hillman implies this when he distinguishes Eros from the other gods and goddesses by saying that Eros is "less a gestalt than a divine function, less a specific pattern than a means of entering into any pattern and coloring it with Eros."[13]

This insight leads into the rest of this work. We begin by approaching the biblical text as Eros, having the power to awaken the preacher's soul or imagination and to eventually lead it into contact with other archetypal powers. When the preacher undergoes the necessary work that brings union with the text, new life will come forth for both preacher and community. The homily that is born from this endeavor can bring joy to others. But more importantly, it is through communion with an imaginal text that one can enter into different worlds of the other archetypes. The image can serve to function in a particular mode or archetypal pattern. In the remainder of the book, we will consider three such patterns or modalities, named after the figures of Apollo, Dionysus, and Hermes. We begin with Apollo.

4.
Imaginal Preaching and Apollo

Apollo who shoots so far...
Lord Phoebus, you who work from a distance...
(Hymn to Pythian Apollo)

An Experience of Apollo

Several years ago I was vacationing in the province of Quebec, Canada and visited St. Joseph's Oratory in Montreal. After viewing the church, I wandered outside and came across the life-sized stations of the cross, carved from great blocks of white stone. I was attracted by their beauty and began to walk among them. The day was overcast, with heavy clouds covering the sun. As I rounded a bend in the path, after the 14th station, the sun suddenly came through a parting in the clouds and I looked upon a 15th station that attempted to capture the risen Christ. The sun hitting it made it dazzling. The body seemed to be emerging from the stone, as if not only transcending but struggling to transform the material from which it was made. There was a strength and power, a pleasing balance and beauty to this image that lifted one's thoughts and feelings. It is this experience I remember as I begin to address one of the archetypal realms that an image, either verbal or visual, can partici-pate in and evoke in others. This realm belongs to Apollo.

To understand what it means to speak of an image functioning as Apollo in preaching, we will first enter his world, captured in story and image. In the various images and stories of Apollo, we find some that

Apollo.

are admirable and some that are not. But let us withhold judgment and simply set them out at first, in order to grasp the entire gestalt that is Apollo. Then we will reflect on how Apollo's world with its distinct feel and values is also part of the preacher's experience, that either we ourselves or others speak out of this archetypal world. Finally, we will try to specify some of the characteristics of an image that works in an Apollonian mode in our consciousness, thereby allowing us to speak of the preaching image as Apollo.

Apollo's World

The images of Apollo will be presented in a series of vignettes. They can be considered a circle of images that interconnect and shed light on each other. You might look upon them as a mosaic, composed of different scenes, which captures this particular pattern of archetypal experience. Apollo cannot be summed up in one story or image; many are needed to capture the complexity and density of his world.

a. *Apollo at Delos.* The small isle of Delos was said to have once floated gently in the Aegean Sea, drifting here and there as the winds allowed. To this island, Leto, pregnant with Apollo and Artemis, came for refuge, fleeing the jealousy of Hera, wife of Zeus. No other city or island would take Leto in, except for Delos. And it was said that this little island became immovably fixed from the moment of Apollo's birth, anchored to the sea bottom by four pillars.

b. *Apollo at Delphi.* Delphi became one of the major shrines of the god. When he was only four days old, Apollo set off in pursuit of the serpent Python who had been chasing his pregnant mother. He cornered him at Delphi and with his bow killed the beast. Set out in the Greek countryside, with hills rising up sharply around it, Apollo's temple at Delphi became a place where people would come to honor Apollo as the god of prophecy. Here many came to consult the Delphic Oracle, presided over by Apollo's priestess, the Pythoness.

c. Apollo the Archer. One of the Homeric hymns begins,

I will remember,
I will not forget
Apollo the Archer.
He goes through this house of Zeus

and he makes the gods tremble.
They all get up, they all get up from their seats
when he comes in,
when he pulls back
his bright bow.[1]

Apollo is frequently portrayed as the archer who shoots so very far, whose aim is perfect, lord of the bow and the straight arrow. Apollo is the one who remains at a distance but who penetrates with his arrow.

d. *Apollo the Healer.* Aesclepius was the son of Apollo and Creusa and it was to him that Apollo taught the art of medicine. Aesclepius used this power to bring a man back to life. When Hades, god of the underworld, heard of this, he was furious and went to Zeus, complaining that he was robbed of one of the dead. Zeus then killed Aesclepius with a thunderbolt. Apollo, furious at this, responded by killing two of Zeus' armor-bearers, the Cyclopes. In punishment, Zeus sent Apollo to work as a shepherd for King Admetus. Here the quiet pastoral life taught him the need for moderation and balance and respect for the rights of the other gods. And so the mature Apollo is known for championing the therapeutic value of moderation in all things. His mottos include, "Nothing in excess" and "Know thyself." The domain of the god of healing includes body, soul, and spirit.

e. *Phoebus Apollo, Hagnos Apollo.* Apollo is linked with the sun and the spirit, the "radiant Apollo" and "the purifying Apollo." He is traditionally a transcendent god, associated with light, brightness, and illumination. He is the giver and interpreter of the law. In Shelley's "Hymn to Apollo," the god announces:

I am the eye with which the Universe
Beholds itself and knows itself divine.

Apollo leads to an awareness of divinity, and calls all to "honor the gods." Christine Downing strikes a balancing note by pointing out that Apollo only gradually became god of law, order, and justice, that earlier on he was a murderer god who needed to be purified, having killed not only the Python but also the two Cyclopes who participated with Zeus in murdering Apollo's son.[2] This reminds us of Apollo's dark side; Apollo can kill.

f. *Apollo and the Muses.* Apollo is leader of the Muses, and so linked with the arts, especially dance, poetry, music and drama. His instrument is the lyre; "the lyre and the bent bow are always going to be loved by me," proclaims Apollo. Harmonious melodies and dignified dance movement characterize his rituals and celebrations.

g. *Apollo and Women.* Apollo's relationship with women is character-ized by rejection and betrayal. His love for Daphne, a water nymph, was unrequited. When Apollo was chasing her and professing his love, she was so resistant to his desires that she called on the earth to swallow her and she was transformed into a laurel tree just as Apollo was within reach. Poor Cassandra, daughter of King Priam of Troy, was foolish enough to promise herself to the god in exchange for the gift of prophe-cy. When she received the gift but refused to honor her promise, Apollo gave her a kiss and spat in her mouth. The result was that no one believed her prophecies, most notably her foreboding one about a wood-en horse placed outside the gates of Troy. Another case was Sibyl, who was promised as many years as there were particles of dust in a pile, and eternal youth besides, but she first toyed with, then spurned the god, and ended up as a punishment living a thousand years, aging all the while, gradually shriveling up until there was only her voice, crying out for release. And, finally, Coronis' infidelity while pregnant with Apollo's son so enraged Apollo that he got his sister Artemis to shoot an arrow through her heart. Later filled with remorse, Apollo sent Hermes to res-cue his child from his mother's womb as she lay on the funeral pyre.

h. *Apollo and Dionysus.* At the shrine at Delphi, there was painted on one side of the temple the image of Apollo, with his mother Leto, his twin sister Artemis, and his handmaidens the nine Muses. Across from this familial portrait was Dionysus, accompanied by the maenads. Apollo not only yielded his temple to Dionysus during the winter months but it is said that he welcomed him, revealing a deep connection between the two which will be taken into account in the next chapter. For now, we wish merely to note their relationship.

Apollo's World, the Preacher's World

The preacher's world often coalesces with the archetypal world of Apollo. We dwell in Apollo when our behavior is rooted in the attitudes and values captured in his images, when our experience draws us into an Apollonian way of looking at things and interacting with others, and when an imaginal text engages our imagination and functions for us in ways that can best be described as Apollonian. Since the Renaissance, Apollo has been called *the* consciousness of western civilization, the embodiment of western culture at its most ideal, with its admiration for his essential attributes of reason, nobility, form, and beauty. Arianna Stassinopoulos says that Hamlet's vision of the human person is rooted in Apollo when he says, "What a piece of work is a man! How noble in reason! how infinite in faculty! in form, in moving, how express and admirable! in action how like an angel! in apprehension how like a god! the beauty of the world!"[3] Before going further, it must be stressed that "to be in Apollo" is not restricted to males, although in the past Apollo's values have been categorized as "masculine." Apollo is a way of being in the world that is related to all, men and women.[4]

When I think of the preacher as a medium for Apollo and his world, I recall the artist Georges Seurat in Stephen Sondheim's stunning musical, *Sunday in the Park with George*. The scene that comes to mind occurs at the end of the first act. We have come to recognize Seurat as an obsessive artist whose entire life is dedicated to his craft; human relationships are simply not a priority. In bits and pieces we have met the people he sketches, including his mistress, his mother, an art critic and his influential wife, two young women and the two soldiers they flirt with, a boatman and his dog, and a few others. We have seen that Seurat is an emotionally detached man, unable to make a commitment to the woman who loves him, kindly but distant toward his mother; he is wed only to his art. All this fits into the Apollonian framework.

Throughout the first act, Seurat is constantly sketching, rearranging again and again his angle of vision. Everyone and everything is constantly shifted about until he achieves a satisfying perspective. He has sketched individuals, couples, pets and trees. At last, all his subjects are in the park on a Sunday. Arguments and accusations have broken out, people are shouting and yelling at each other, moving toward and away from one another. It is a scene of total chaos. Suddenly, Seurat stops and shouts out over the cacophony, "Order!" Everyone quiets and turns to him. He looks at them, nods to one, then another, controlling without touching, at a distance, beckoning them into the final arrangement.

The people start to move in a slow circular procession as Seurat calls

out in a clear, firm voice: "Design...Tension...Balance...Harmony..."
And as they move in a stately flow, they begin to sing. It is a beautiful,
harmonious hymn, solemnly liturgical and majestic. The artist moves
about arranging and rearranging trees, animals, and people one last
time, until finally he steps back in satisfaction. For the viewer, all the
life bursting forth on the stage has come together into a fixed reproduction of Seurat's masterpiece, "A Sunday Afternoon on the Island of the
Grand Jatte." As the concluding notes of the hymn sounded and a frame
came down and embraced the now still image, there was a moment of
silence. All was frozen in a state of ordered perfection.

It was certainly one of the most satisfying moments in the theater that
I can ever remember. I had experienced a movement from chaos to creation, from disorder and disruption to balance and beauty. Significantly,
the song that accompanied this was an evocative, harmonious hymn
called "Sunday." How fitting for Apollo, god of the sun. I have often
thought of this moment in the theater when I think of the preacher as an
artist who participates in and evokes the world of Apollo. On Sunday we
are called to stand before our communities, who have come into the temple of worship from the chaos of life, and who want to hear a word that
might bring order, balance, harmony to their world, enabling a visitation
of the archetypal force we name Apollo. Again, bear in mind that this is a
mode of psychologizing about what is happening within the imagination
in its relationship with the images that speak and mediate the God of
Israel revealed in Christ.

The domain of Apollo reveals a gestalt of qualities which can be
related to the task of preaching. The images that are given in the myth
are helpful here. One of the first images associated with Apollo is his
place of birth, Delos, an island swimming in the Aegean, which at the
moment of the god's birth strikes roots in the foundations of the sea.
Apollo is the power that brings stability. Just as this island moves from
flowing to fixed because of Apollo's presence, so Apollo brings a certain immovable and settled quality wherever he is found.

We can translate this event into a more psychological framework by
speaking of the "heroic ego," with its fixed perspective on the world, its
need to subdue any restlessness and disorder. The Apollonian perspective provides and insists on a sense of order, harmony, and balance. This
aspect of a clear, single-minded vision is also captured in the image of

Apollo the archer, the one who shoots from afar, penetrating whatever he aims at with his arrow. The archer image also contains that sense of distance so characteristic of this god, the distance of objectivity, a deliberate refraining from any emotional attachment.

Walter Otto, a scholar of myth, writes of the knowledge that Apollo brings by saying that the god "objects to extreme proximity"; such closeness causes a blurred gaze which results in a loss of clarity. "In Apollo," he says, "we encounter the spirit of observable knowledge."[5] It is easy to see how Apollo became the guiding spirit of the scientific age; his gift was knowledge that was detached, precise, objective. Such characteristics are carried over into religion and the world of preaching when priority is given to imparting knowledge of the faith, guiding principles, dogmatic assertions; when preaching style is marked by syllogistic clarity, penetrating analysis, and grounded, when possible, in objective knowledge and scientifically based facts; when preachers turn to source books such as catechisms and dictionaries as compendiums of knowledge that inform their preaching. In this kind of preaching, a community will know the stability and security that faith can provide.

Apollo's world is the world of heights and peaks. Hillman says that

peaks have belonged to the spirit ever since Mount Sinai and Mount Olympus, Mount Patmos and the Mount of Olives, and Mount Moriah of the first patriarchal Abraham. And you will easily name a dozen other mountains of the spirit. It does not require much explication to realize that the peak experience is a way of describing pneumatic experience, and that the clamber up the peaks is in search of the spirit or is the drive of the spirit in search of itself.[6]

Apollo's titles of Phoebus (radiant, clarifying) and Hagnos (holy, purifying) link him with the sun and with the world of spirit. As Phoebus, Apollo clarifies, brings light, drying out what is moist, making it firm and solid. Apollo is the ascending movement, the upward thrust, revealing full power at the zenith. As Hagnos, Apollo is the pure, holy, cleansing god. Such aspects connect us with the transcendence that is very much a value in Apollo's world; the One who is far above is truly "other" and apart.

When Thomas Troeger writes that in preaching we help people to "climb up into the truths of their lives," he is speaking of the preaching archetypally located in the world of Apollo. The upward climb brings perspective, clarity, distance from the chaos, the murky, dark, wet world in which everything is in flux and open to dissolution. The upward climb into the pulpit, so common in the past, concretely captured this dimension, as the preacher moved toward the high place of the church, where he would offer a word that clarified, purified, and inspired, allowing the soul to transcend its earthly cares.

Preaching can enliven and enlighten the spirit. Apollo points to a preaching that is prophetic, therapeutic, and "coolly" aesthetic. As the god of prophecy, Apollo reminds us of our need for a word that opens up the present and offers new and renewing possibilities. The shrine at Delphi was a place where the priestess, speaking out of what Plato called a "prophetic madness," offered creative insights which were often quite cryptic. Rollo May makes an interesting comment on this. First, he says that "the sayings of the shrine, like dreams, were not to be received passively; *the recipients had to 'live' themselves into the message*" (italics mine); he further explains that "the effect of ambiguous prophecies was to force the suppliants to think out their situation anew, to reconsider their plans, and to conceive of new possibilities."[7]

Preaching's participation in the prophetic role remains an important part of our tradition. Walter Brueggemann has written of the prophetic imagination that offers "an alternative construal of reality." This is a vision that both criticizes the status quo and offers another version of reality that God's people are called to "live themselves into" by the power of the Spirit. When we engage in prophetic preaching we are under the archetypal power of Apollo.

Apollo also links the language of preaching to healing, as he is the god concerned with the healing of the community. There was an awareness in the classical Greek world that healing power was to be found in a form of speech called the "epode." In his work on this subject, Pedro Lain Entralgo[8] discusses how Plato wrote of this form of speech as having power to charm the soul. The epode was an imaginal form: a tale, a myth, or an example. Entralgo describes it as a "suggestive word [that] can be called a charm whenever it is 'beautiful speech' and when as a result it produces in the soul, *sophrosyne*, beautiful, harmonious, and rightful ordering of all the ingredients of life: beliefs, feelings, impulses,

knowledge, thoughts and value judgments."[9] Beauty, harmony, order—
we are in the realm of Apollo.

The condition of sophrosyne was a healing condition to be achieved
either by a reordering of the contents of the soul around active beliefs
already present or by eliciting new beliefs more noble than the old.[10] For
Plato this was the function of what he called "mythical language" over
against "discursive reasoning." And this mythical language was the language of story and image, poetic tools whose importance has been
recently recovered by preaching. When the preacher uses images, stories to effect a harmonious balance in the soul, the healing power of
Apollo is operative.

Walker Percy wrote from a slightly different yet related perspective
of the healing power of language when he spoke of the "diagnostic
novel."[11] For Percy the healing of the modern spiritual malaise eroding
our life as a people must begin with an accurate diagnosis of the situation, an understanding based on a clear perception and knowledge of
what was wrong. Percy saw that the primary business of both literature
and art was to be cognitive: to find out, know and tell the name of the
"dis-ease" that afflicts modern life. This call for a diagnosis that would
bring knowledge and clarity placed Percy's vision of the novel under the
aegis of Apollo. When preaching provides such a diagnosis, a similar
naming of the "dis-ease" that torments us, it is also functioning in this
perspective of the god of healing, healing effected by clarity, knowledge, and objective discernment—the gifts of Apollo.

The images of Apollo, then, conjure up a definite archetypal world
that can be related to a particular type of preaching. These same hallmark qualities of the Apollonian world can be used as guidelines when
we approach the task of bringing an imaginal text into the life of the
community which has gathered for worship. People come to hear a
word of life; the archetype of Apollo offers a particular approach to how
an imaginal text might bring that word.

Preaching's Image as Apollo

Before discussing the specifics of considering a particular image or
text from an Apollonian perspective, a few general comments. When we
approach a biblical text from any archetypal perspective, there should
be no intent to manipulate the text so that its own particular context is

violated. All the usual study that goes into the preparation for preaching on a biblical text is to take place. When this is finished as part of the process of entering into the world of the passage, when we have achieved union of soul and text, then we can ask certain questions that flow from various archetypal perspectives which we wish to consider. The imaginal text might function one time from an Apollonian perspective, at another from the Dionysian, Hermetic, or some other. Several perspectives might be considered in preparation and perhaps even more than one might be employed in the actual preaching. For clarity's sake we will consider one perspective at a time.

Secondly, it is also true that a certain text or an entire book might seem to align itself more with one perspective than another. For instance, when I think of Apollo's world and its values, I find it very congruent with Matthew's gospel. The first gospel contains certain images, themes, even a certain "feel" that are reflective of this archetypal sphere. Just as Apollo's concern is with giving and presenting the law of Zeus, Matthew's Jesus is presented as one who ascends the mountain to give a sermon that articulates the new law of the kingdom. "You have heard...but I say to you..." is a refrain we hear again and again. Jesus proclaims that he is the one who comes to fulfill the law, saying that not one jot or one tittle will be lost, and that the person who accepts this teaching will be like one who builds a house on stone. The stability characteristic of Apollo is also the gift of Jesus to those who take his yoke upon them. Simon's name is changed to Peter, meaning "rock," and on this rock rests the church.

Other Apollonian qualities can be found throughout Matthew. This gospel stresses that Jesus not only fulfills the law but also the prophets. Matthew quotes numerous prophets in his presentation of Jesus. Jesus is also the healer, lifting up the daughter of Jairus, telling others to pick up their mats and walk. He is the teacher through his parables and extended discourses. Jesus calls on his followers to be light for the world, a city placed on a hilltop. The high place as the realm of spirit is evoked not only in Jesus' sermon on the mount but also by his taking Peter, James and John up onto a very high mountain where the transfiguration occurs, and by his final appearance to the eleven disciples in Galilee on a mountain. All this imagery is resonant with the world of Apollo.

Finally, Matthew's world is predominantly male. Emphasis is placed on the special position of the twelve, who are treated far more favorably than they are in Mark's gospel. The opening infancy narrative is centered on Joseph, through whom Jesus is linked with the house of David. The relationship with women is more distant here. Compared with Luke's gospel, women play a more secondary role. Matthew presents a predominantly patriarchal world in which both the friends and enemies of Jesus were men; women are mostly at the periphery. This is also characteristic of the world of Apollo.

But even though we might be able to identify a certain archetypal influence within a particular gospel or book of the Bible, I would propose that *any* text can be approached from an Apollonian perspective and its images can be crafted out of that particular world's influence. There are questions that a homilist can ask when approaching biblical images through an Apollonian lens. Making use of the gospel (Mt 28:1-10) for the Easter vigil in the Roman lectionary, cycle A, I offer the following questions rooted in the archetype of Apollo.

A. How can the images of this text *enlighten* our lives as a community? What particular darkness do they dispel?

James Hillman has written that there are times when Apollo is utterly essential, "when you need an ideal image for orientation. Sometimes the soul needs discipline and wants sunshine, clear and distinct ideas."[12] Perhaps a need for an "ideal image for orientation," for clarity, for clear and distinct ideas can be met when you ask how a particular image offers this to the community.

Shortly I will present a homily that I preached this past Easter. When I looked for an ideal image for orientation on the feast of new fire, of paschal light, the gospel for the Easter vigil presented the community with an angel who rolls away the rock, creating an earthquake, and, with Roman soldiers cowering like dead men, it delivers the good news of Easter, sitting on the same stone that had blocked entry. This is an image that orients, that points us toward the rising Sun, the Holy One who has been raised. The light of this figure, like the light that seemed to emanate from the marble sculpture of the risen Christ in the gardens of St. Joseph's Oratory, can be used to enlighten minds and hearts on such an occasion.

Such an image disciplines (from the Latin *disciplina*, a teaching) and makes us disciples, thereby revealing to us who we are, in fulfillment of the Apollonian admonition, "Know thyself." The act of rolling away the rock can be seen as pivotal for our entry into the place of Jesus' resurrection. The Easter angel instructs us in knowledge that he is risen, and that we are not to be afraid. "He has been raised exactly as he promised." Clarity, warm like the sun, an ideal image that orients us toward fullness of life—this is the *disciplina*, the instruction, that serves as a foundation for self-awareness.

B. How can this text offer us a glimpse of the *holy*, take us more deeply into the *mystery*? How can it function to *lift* us to a higher place?

Apollo's movement is upward, toward the heights. He is the god of spirit, of transcendence. The angel's proclamation that he has been raised moves us upward into the power of spirit. And we are called by our faith to see and live in the power of spirit. What does this mean for this community? In what ways are they being called to hear the voice of the angel that tells them not to fear? What is the rock that needs to be moved so that they can enter into Easter faith?

Flannery O'Connor speaks of the need to suggest mystery through manners, what is unseen through what is seen. She writes that it is possible for our words to give birth to an "anagogical vision."[13] By this she means "the kind of vision that is able to see different levels of reality in one image or situation." That kind of vision refers to divine life and our participation in it. By working through some of the details, the "manners" that a text offers, one looks for what provides entry into a sense of mystery. The text begins as the first day of the week is dawning, with women moving toward a place that holds only death. Do these figures speak to a community that moves toward the dawn, offering the promise of God's power to raise what is thought to be dead?

C. How does the text offer *healing*? Does it contain an image that diagnoses our condition or offers hope of cure?

By featuring certain images of the gospel, we can attempt to provide an instance of the Platonic *epode*, beautiful speech offering balance, harmony, healing for the soul. The Easter images are from the climactic moment of the Judaeo-Christian story, *the* myth, that helps to order our beliefs, feelings, thoughts and values. What is in need of healing for the community that has come together? How can these images speak to it? Is there room here for further diagnosis of our illness, so we might understand it and realize our need for the transcending power of this angel and the energizing message of leaving the place of death and going out into the light to bring light?

D. How does the imaginal text offer *prophetic insight*? Brueggemann's "construal of an alternative world" is offered in this gospel as a world in which angels come with fear-lifting messages and enlist us in the messenger corps. The entry into the tomb is paradoxical. Only by going into the place of death can new life come about. An alternative world can also be found through the use of the other readings for the vigil—readings that speak of a world of new creation, obedience, freedom, a world of covenant, conversion, wisdom, in which we will be given new spirits and new hearts. How does the specific imagery of the texts offer a new vision and critique the present world in which we live?

Madeleine L'Engle offers a biblical spirituality to the artist when she says that the task of the writer is to bring "cosmos out of chaos" and to fashion "icons of the true."[14] This is also an Apollonian vision. From the richness of biblical imagery, the preacher offers a cosmos in which the community can come to see themselves as whole. Such images function as icons that set us free from other images that limit and constrict. The biblical world is one in which angels continue to move huge stones and proclaim life in the place of darkness and death.

We must not neglect the shadow side of Apollo when we consider the image from this perspective. Hillman interprets the tales of Apollo's failure with women as warning us that to move in the world of Apollo can be devastating to the psyche or soul, even while it is good for the spirit. He suggests that such qualities as emotion, imagination, and even intuition can be neglected in the world of Apollo, whose primary attributes include clarity of thought, abstract synthesis, detachment, and lack of involvement.

A case can be made that much of our past preaching has fallen under Apollo's archetypal influence, since so much emphasis was placed on being instructional and attending to the needs of the spirit. But such needs are legitimate. However, the climb to the pulpit in the past had the effect of making people feel distant from the preacher, placing him on high, while they were struggling down below. There was a certain Apollonian tone to some preaching that seemed more the material of official documents which often neglect the soul's love of image. As with all the archetypes, this one has its shadow, but there is much present in this perspective that is to be valued.

From the four questions above, one can then move to crafting a homily that features the images of the text while allowing them to be reworked by one's own imagination and amplified by the images of one's own experience. The following is a homily given at an Easter Vigil service. It tried to honor not only the images of the gospel but also some of the other nine readings that were heard. It was developed out of an Apollonian perspective.

Removing the Stone

Eugene LaVerdiere tells a wonderful story about a first grade class
    that was putting on an Easter pageant.
The production was to be performed numerous times throughout the
    school, concluding with the presentation before the pastor and
    parents.
One little boy was asked to play the huge stone that seals the tomb.
During each performance, during the appropriate time, he would roll
    across the stage.
After a number of performances, his concerned teacher asked if he
    would like to be something else for one of the performances—
    a soldier perhaps or even Joseph of Aramathea.
"Nope," said the boy. He liked being the rock.
When it was all over, the teacher asked, "Why did you enjoy so
    much playing a rock?"
"I loved the moment," he said, "when I rolled across and let Jesus
    out of the tomb."

It was a child's understanding of the rock, says LaVerdiere.
The boy correctly understood that the rock had a function in the
    gospel.
He didn't understand exactly what it was.
It is not so much that the rock stops Jesus from getting out of the
    tomb.
It is more a matter of the rock stopping others from entering.
The rock is whatever prevents us from entering the tomb,
    from dying and being buried with Christ.

On this night of nights, we can ask a question.
On this night of renewal, when we recommit ourselves by renewing
    our baptismal promises, we can raise this question.
What prevents me from dying with Christ so that I can rise?
What prevents us as a community from dying and being buried with
    him?

What is my stone? our stone?
Secrets that keep us nailed to a cross.
Secret abuse we perform or tolerate or ignore.
Secret judgments on which we build our lives, judgments that size
    up, diminish, and dismiss others.
Secret hatreds and prejudices nurtured and nourished
        against blacks, hispanics, whites, rich, poor, gays, straights,...
What is the stone that keeps us out of Easter life?

Who will roll back the stone that prevents us from entering the
    tomb?
The One who was there from the beginning and whose past acts
    continue to occur for us.
The One who sent the Spirit over
        chaos and now sends the Spirit
        once again to move over our hearts.
The One who called Abraham to obedience
        and now calls us to listen to the divine will:
        that no more children,
        be they unborn,
        or the children of the inner cities
        or the children of the poor nations,
        that none be sacrificed.
The One who led Moses and the people through the sea
        and now calls us to know true freedom by sacrificing
        so that the poor
        will have more, even at our expense.
The One who called Israel to conversion and covenant
        and to true wisdom
        and who will shout until we hear that same call in our
        lives.

The One who promised a new heart and a new spirit
  and who will send that gift to all of us,
    but especially those who are being baptized tonight.

Who will roll back the stone for us?
An angel of the Lord proclaims this night,
    "Don't be frightened."
    Don't be frightened of those who can harm your body but not
      your soul.
    Don't be frightened of those who choose to put their trust in
      their own strength.
    Don't be frightened because those who are willing to die in
      Christ will truly live.
Go and tell your brothers and sisters that the Lord has risen and that
    he will meet you in your own lives.
He will meet you where you work and live and love.
He has been raised.
Lifted up to new life.
And *that* is our destiny. Amen. Alleluia.

Apollo is one archetypal world which can influence how we craft an
image in preaching. I have mentioned that the shrine of Apollo at
Delphi was given over for several months of each year to his half-brother Dionysus. This figure is as far away from the god of reason, moderation, and balance as is possible, and yet it is said that Apollo welcomed
him. Let us now turn to this figure.

5.
Imaginal Preaching and Dionysus

Is anything brighter than the sun?
Yet it can be eclipsed. (Sir 17:26)

An Experience of Dionysus

In 1985 I was out at Berkeley at the Pacific School of Religion and walked into one of the campus buildings to find myself suddenly falling into a different psychic space. Looking about, I saw up on the wall a sculpted image called *Christa*, the crucified Christ embodied as a woman, at once voluptuous and writhing in pain. I can remember a rush of feeling going through me at the time. Shock. Fascination. Confusion. Anger. "Now what's this all about? What's the agenda?" I found myself saying—to myself, of course, trying to put this in its proper place. The familiar had been turned upside down and I was in an unfamiliar place, acutely aware of its strangeness. I had seen many cultural expressions of the crucifixion, but none like this.

At a later time, I was reading a book and came across the lines, "We are an Apollonian people living in an Apollonian civilization. Or so we think until Dionysus rises from the depths and tears the Apollonian order asunder."[1] One way to interpret my experience was as a sudden shift in worlds. For a moment, my clear, orderly, logical, Apollonian world had been upended. I had been taken somewhere else.

The world of Dionysus is often viewed as being at the other end of

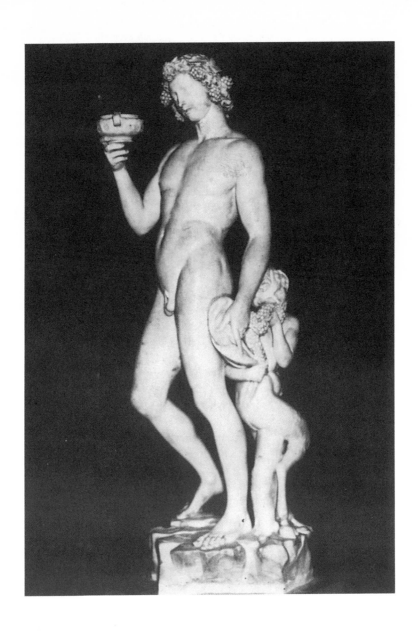

Dionysus.

the spectrum from the world of Apollo. And yet, the two are half-broth-
ers, sons of Zeus. And in ancient times for three months every year
Apollo was said to leave his temple at Delphi in favor of his brother.
What necessity does this point to? We know and live in Apollo very
comfortably. Now it is time to ponder the archetypal world that
Dionysus can suddenly thrust upon us.

Dionysus' World

Various images from the myth of Dionysus provide the best introduction to this archetypal pattern and its distinct perspective.

a. *Dionysus' Double Birth.* Hera, wife of Zeus, was both angry and
jealous of the pregnant Semele; for the father of the child was Zeus. Out
of revenge, Hera urged this mortal daughter of King Cadmus and Queen
Harmonia to beg Zeus to show himself in the fullness of his power.
Unfortunately, Semele liked the idea. Shortly thereafter, when Zeus
offered to grant Semele whatever she wished, she made this request.
Held by his promise, Zeus reluctantly complied and Semele was
instantly consumed by the power of his bolts of lightning—but not
before Zeus was able to seize the child from her womb and sew him
into his own thigh, carrying him there for the remaining three months of
pregnancy. Thus, Dionysus is called "twice-born" and "child of the double doors." He was born of mother and of father, of human and divine
parentage. His name is said to mean "Zeus' limp," for that is how Zeus
walked during the time he carried him in his thigh.

b. *The Mad Dionysus.* Cursed by Hera, Dionysus wandered the land
in a state of madness and drew others into it. As a child, Hera caused
those who were entrusted with his upbringing to go mad so they would
try to kill him. Again and again Dionysus narrowly escaped death. As
an adult, he prowled the woods, as hunter and hunted, persecutor and
persecuted. The god was once cast into a bottomless lake by Perseus,
and, at another time, driven into the watery depths by Lycurgus—thus
his association with what is dark and wet. His ability to draw others into
madness is captured in his conflict with Pentheus. When this Greek
king opposed the god, Dionysus set on him a group of his frenzied maenads (the women who followed him), led by the king's own mother, and
they dismembered him. But there is also another side to Dionysus' madness which links it with ecstasy.

c. *Dionysus and the Maenads.* Dionysus is a god of community; especially to be noted is his association with women. Paintings show him wandering through the woods accompanied by the maenads, women who have left their traditional roles and become companions of the god. One of the names given to Dionysus is *Lysios,* the Loosener, for he called women from their marriages and duties at home to join him outside the city walls. With their heads thrown back and wreathed with ivy, they joined with Dionysus in his revels and wild ways. Sometimes they suckled the wild beasts; sometimes they dismembered them. The maenads were portrayed with Dionysus on the pediment opposite Apollo at the Shrine of Delphi.

d. *The Dismembered Dionysus.* Dionysus' suffering begins in his childhood. When very young, he was surrounded by a group of the Titans, a race of giants, who tore him to pieces, and boiled him in a cauldron. His grandmother Rhea came along, recovered the pieces, and restored him. This same Rhea would later purify Dionysus of the many violent murders he committed while mad and introduce him to the sacred mysteries. Another version of his dismemberment says that Zeus gave the limbs of the dismembered god to Apollo who took them to Delphi.

e. *Dionysus and the Underworld.* An alternative version of his birth has him born of Persephone and Zeus in a dark cave, earning him the name "Chthonios," meaning "the subterranean one" and linking him with the underworld. Other than Hades, he is associated more with death than any other god. This link with the underworld further explains his association with darkness and descent into the depths. Another of his names is the Lord of Souls.

f. *Dionysus and the Earth.* Dionysus has a strong connection with the earth, including the world of vegetation and of animals. As Apollo is the god of the peaks, Dionysus is found in the shadowy, wet places, in the vales and valleys. The vine, ivy, myrtle, fig and pine tree belong to him, and all trees that bear fruit. He also claims the lion, panther, and bull, among other animals. He is associated with moisture and life-giving fluids, such as the sap of trees and plants, milk and wine. In Michelangelo's famous bronze statue in the Bargello in Florence, Dionysus, under the Roman name Bacchus, is portrayed as the intoxicated god, full of wine and good cheer.

g. *Dionysus and the Mysteries.* Dionysus is connected with the worship of the mysteries in the temple and with mysticism. When he entered the temple, his music was the impassioned choric hymn and the dancing of his followers was wild and frenzied. At his appearance in the temple, vines begin to grow, wine spills forth, milk and honey flow.

h. *Dionysus, God of Epiphany and Transformation.* Another hallmark is that he appears and disappears suddenly; he also assumes many different shapes. While the Titans were attacking him, he changed himself from a child to a snake, then a lion, and finally a bull. One of the Homeric hymns records how he appeared once as a young man walking on the promontory of the sea. Not knowing who he was, pirates captured him, planning to hold him for ransom, but the ropes with which they attempted to bind him to the mast would not hold. Suddenly, wine began to bubble over the deck, and the mast was wrapped with vines and ivy. Dionysus was transformed into a lion, and then a bear also appeared. When the lion turned on the captain, the rest of the crew jumped overboard and were changed into dolphins. Only the helmsman who had tried to defend the god was spared and rewarded.

i. *Dionysus and Women.* Much of Dionysus' childhood was spent hiding from Hera; during this time he was dressed and educated as a girl. He is sometimes portrayed as effeminate. But his relationship with women is markedly different from that of Apollo or from any other god. Jean Shinoda Bolen says that this divinity is "the only god who rescues and restores (instead of dominating or raping) women."[2] The maenads followed him faithfully. He went down into the underworld and brought his mother Semele up to Olympus, obtaining immortality for her. When he came upon Ariadne, abandoned by Theseus on the isle of Naxos, he married her, winning immortality for her also. And, unlike many of the other Greek divinities, he was a faithful husband. It is easy to understand why his cult was so popular with women.

The above images point to a realm easily distinguishable from Apollo's, containing both madness and mysticism, dismemberment and renewal, the masculine and the feminine, rapture and terror. While Apollo invites us upward to the high places, Dionysus calls us to the depths. We will consider how Dionysus' world is also the preacher's world.

Dionysus' World, the Preacher's World

How does Dionysus come into our world? What does he bring about in life that allows us to name an experience as Dionysian? What are the hallmarks of being "in" Dionysus. Another example from the world of theater may be helpful. Peter Shaffer's play *Equus*[3] opens with an adolescent boy, Alan Strang, being brought to a psychiatrist, Martin Dysart. The boy has used a steel spike to blind six horses. The question is why? The magistrate who brings the boy to Dysart pleads that he take the boy on as a patient, for the other judges are appalled by the barbarous act he has committed and seem inclined to punish him severely. Dysart reluctantly agrees to the request and in the subsequent encounters with Alan Strang we, along with Dysart, begin to enter into a world transformed by a visitation from Dionysus.

The play unfolds like a mystery with Dysart as a detective trying to understand what led up to the evening in the stable and the brutal blinding of the horses. Like many other horrible events, this sudden explosion is rooted in the past to some degree, especially in the history of a particular person, but, perhaps most of all, in the mystery of life itself. As Dysart confesses in one of his monologues:

> ...A child is born into a world of phenomena all equal in their power to enslave. It sniffs—it sucks—it strokes its eyes over the whole uncomfortable range. Suddenly one strikes. Why? Moments snap together like magnets, forging a chain of shackles. Why? I can trace them. I can even, with time, pull them apart again. But why at the start they were ever magnetized at all—just those particular moments of experience and no others—I don't know. *And nor does anyone else....*[4]

Dysart rightly perceives that there is a mysterious power at work here which is not to be easily and rationally pinned down.

The boy's first significant encounter with the power embodied as Equus occurred on a beach when he was six. A man lifted Alan onto his horse, and as the boy began to ride, he cried out, "Bear me away." This command proves to be prophetic. Strang's mother recounts to Dysart that, when Alan was little, he would beg her to read repeatedly a story about a horse whose only rider was his young master; she also notes that he had a great love for westerns. All this seems quite normal. A stranger turn occurred later, she notes, on an occasion involving a picture that Alan's father forced on him when he was twelve. It portrayed a horse from a head on perspective; "it comes out all eyes," says the mother. In reaction to his wife's religiosity, the father made his son replace a picture of Christ on the way to Calvary with that of the horse. In an interview with Dysart, the father recalls how one night he came upon the boy kneeling naked before it, chanting a nonsensical genealogy, apparently worshiping before it, as he whipped himself with a metal coat hanger. The climax of the first act has Alan himself reliving for Dysart a surreptitious midnight ride at a stable where he worked. At the darkest hour, under the moon, boy and horse are galloping over the fields, joined in a seemingly mystical—if not mad—bond: "Feel me on you. *On* you! *On* you! *On* you! I want to be *in* you. I want to BE you forever and ever! *Equus, I love you*! Now! Bear me away! Make us one person!"

Over against Alan's intense turmoil is the spell that the psychiatrist himself falls under. He is intrigued by what has happened to the boy, confessing his jealousy. Dysart, an admirer of the ancient civilization of Greece, describes himself as "lost," "desperate," "all reined up in old language and old assumptions, straining to jump clean-hoofed on to a whole new track of being I only suspect is there." Dysart recognizes there is a mystery here drawing ever closer, lapping at the borders of his own consciousness, defying the logic, clarity, and control that the Apollonian world imposes, and confronting his own impotence to "solve" things:

> Now he's (i.e., Alan Strang) gone off to rest, leaving me alone with Equus. I can hear the creature's voice. It's calling me out of the black cave of the Psyche. I shove in my dim little torch, and there he stands, waiting for me. He raises his matted head. He opens his great square teeth and says—(mocking) "Why?...Why Me?...Why—ultimately—Me?...Do you really imagine you can account for Me? Totally, infallibly, inevitably account for Me?...Poor Doctor Dysart!"[5]

The mystery behind the blinding of the horses is finally brought into the open and addressed, or—more accurately, reduced—in a way that brings the boy back into the comfort of the conventional world. But is the cure truly a cure? Dysart's hesitant agreement to restore the boy to "normality" through the somewhat facile use of a placebo and his subsequent outburst invite the audience to share in the ambiguity of such a "cure":

> *All right! All right! I'll take it away!* He'll be delivered from madness. *What then?* He'll feel himself acceptable! *What then?* Do you think feelings like his can be simply re-attached, like plasters? Stuck on to other objects we select? *Look at him!*...My desire might be to make this boy an ardent husband—a caring citizen—a worshiper of an abstract and unifying God. My achievement, however, is more likely to make a ghost!...[6]

The play takes us beyond the comfortable and conforming borders of our world to one that is violent, upsetting, mad, yet filled with passion, wonder, ecstasy, and worship between a young man and this "other" called "Equus." There is dismemberment, both in the mutilation of the horses and in the excision of Equus from Strang's soul. We also witness union, terror and rapture. In the young man's androgynous look and his relationship with Equus, we find masculine and feminine intertwined. Dionysus enters the everyday world, and for Alan Strang, it—and he—is torn apart and transformed. Shaffer's play effectively captures many aspects of the archetypal world of Dionysus and invites our reflection on how it intersects with our own. There are three salient features found in varying degrees in the play that have been identified as essential to Dionysus: madness, dismemberment, and bisexuality. Let us consider what implications they have for preachers.

First of all, Dionysus brings "madness." The classicist Walter F. Otto considers this aspect the god's essential feature. He speaks of it in a most positive, and perhaps most romantic, vein when he writes:

> The madness which is called Dionysus is no sickness, no debility in life, but a companion of life at its healthiest. It is the tumult which erupts from the innermost recesses when they mature and force their way to the surface. It is the madness inherent in the womb of the mother. This attends all moments of creation, constantly changes ordered existence into chaos, and ushers in primal

salvation and primal pain—and in both, the primal wildness of
being.[7]

The madness of the god that Otto speaks of here is the power of the life
force, what the Greeks called Zoe. It is unbridled, undifferentiated life,
that brings bliss, rapture, ecstasy and intoxication. But Dionysian life is
also linked with dismemberment, darkness and death. To be under the
influence of this god is to be caught up in passionate enthusiasm, and
to feel oneself to be an instrument through which life flows and surges.
But this calls for a dying; it is a dying to the placid, neat, comfortable
places where we live with little change in the emotional thermometer,
where we are in control; it can also be a dying to much that we love
and hold dear.

Perhaps the moments we know Dionysus best in his most positive
form are those times of creativity, when "the juices" are flowing
through us, when there is a sense of being taken over. These can occur
when we are alone, working, and something suddenly strikes, for
Dionysus arrives suddenly, or during the creative moment of performance when one "lets go," when there is the feeling of being close to
both life and death, of both being on the edge and falling, of abandon-
ing oneself to the life force that is too powerful to resist. Perhaps you
know those times before getting up to preach when it is difficult to
move; one senses nearness to the edge, then one pushes off and dives
into the moment. Again, Otto says,

> He who begets something which is alive must dive down into the
> primeval depths in which the forces of life dwell. And when he
> rises to the surface, there is a gleam of madness in his eyes
> because in those depths death lives cheek by jowl with life.[8]

Dionysus is the god who dissolves the boundaries between life and
death; when he is present, so are they. But let us look closer at the kind
of dying Dionysus brings about.

The destruction Dionysus causes has to do with dismemberment and
dissolution, but not primarily on a physical level. Dionysus is torn apart
early on in the myth, and, as an adult, comes to be called Lysios, the
Loosener, because he then tears apart the social order. Plato links this
social rending with Dionysus' madness when he discusses two kinds of

madness, one related to sickness, the other arising from "a supernatural release from the conventions of life."[9] The images of releasing from the conventions of life as a kind of madness are most notably associated with the god's call to women to leave their enclosed lives and to wander the hills with him and join in his music, madness, and mystical revels. He called them to a freedom that threatened the social structure of Greek society. Women have been portrayed as entering into the "madness" of the god, but Christine Downing reflects that the only women who truly went mad were the ones who resisted him; the rest formed a ritual community, a *thiasos*, excluding men, where they worshiped the god as a group, and came to know the exhilaration that comes with the release of pent-up instinctual energies.[10] Dionysus was also said to be beloved of all who were slaves, for he represented the liberation of those most enchained. His archetypal world is one in which the oppressed know freedom.

The preacher concerned with loosening and liberating those who are constricted by the stability of social conventions enters into Dionysus' realm. And this will mean the possibility of being torn apart by those who oppose this interference and threat. "Dionysus dismembered" continues in those who would speak against the powerful who are wedded to the status quo. Yet preachers are called to work wherever liberation is necessary from those things that stifle spirit and kill the soul; their words and images can stir up the force of life in the hearts of those dying enchained.

Finally, Dionysus is strongly linked with androgyny and bisexuality, adding to the unsettling effect his influence has on those who encounter him in whatever form. He erases the boundaries between male and female, and what is traditionally called "masculinity" and "femininity," in his own person. He is called both "the phallic one" and "the womanly one." He is both a strongly virile figure wedded to Ariadne, rescuer of women, opposing oppressive order, and an effeminate figure who was raised and dressed as a girl in childhood, who lacks true virility, who carries a detached phallus. He is called "the hybrid" and "the man-woman." This aspect is hardly comfortable or comforting. Yet Hillman sees in this particular quality the essence of the god. In contrast with Apollo, Dionysus brings a consciousness in which there is no misogyny because "it is not divided from its own femininity."[11] Dionysus represents a bisexual or androgynous consciousness not as one in which the female has been added or integrated into the dominant male consciousness but one "where male and female are primordially united. The *coniunctio* is not an attainment but a given. It is not a goal to be sought but an a priori possibility, always there for everyone."[12]

Dionysus brings psychological bisexuality, an androgyny in which what has formerly been attributed to masculinity and femininity is now recognized as belonging to all. For Hillman that means a human consciousness in which not only intuition, emotion, and the world of nature—all traditionally assigned to the realm of "the feminine"—are included, but also such experiences as incompleteness, imperfection, passivity, dependence, introvertedness, interiority, and even depression are accepted and valued. The Apollonian quest for success, perfection, action, and extraversion, and all other signs of the heroic, traditionally "masculine" order are components of only one world, not *the* world. Dionysian madness, dissolution, bisexuality belong to another. Hillman sees entry, whether willing or forced, into the Dionysian as an invitation to consciousness to "unthink its long identification with only male qualities" and "to take back into itself the physical, the feminine, and the inferior."[13]

Where do we find the Dionysian today? We hear his voice in those who call for new images of God, who speak from and for the world of women, the world of gays and lesbians, the third world, and the world of ecological concern. In these places one hears voices that challenge our certainty about the social, the sexual, and the theological underpinnings we have grown to think of as unassailable. We hear voices questioning what is necessary and what is expendable, what is superior and inferior, what is life-giving and death-dealing. We can hardly intuit all that our participation in the psychological realm of this mad, wild, dismembered, bisexual god might have in store for the future regeneration of life.

What does this mean for preaching? The world of Dionysus brings back to preaching a respect for the world of the feminine and the world of matter, a regard for the mystical madness that detonates our comfortable categories. It goes against the prejudice that truth is more present in the spirit realm of concepts and abstractions than in the images and stories that spring from our material world, the world of matter that matters. Dionysus calls us to be open to ecstasy, intoxication, and rapture. He also invites us to honor the incomplete, the inner images that come to us unbidden, the darkness that suddenly falls upon our work. This archetypal presence reminds us that preaching that has too little to do with emotion and distrusts intuition will only serve to keep the soul at a distance. He calls for preaching that allows a people to enter into the mystery as a community, not just as individuals, and a preaching that is concerned with the people who are on the margins, the fringes, the edges of contemporary life.

The Dionysian combines what has been divided into masculine and feminine, the active and passive, life and death, and destruction and rebirth. Alongside the Apollonian emphasis on ascent, light, integration, the heroic, it brings descent, darkness, dissolution, and even death. Such preaching lacks the certainty of the Apollonian mode with its clarity and sense of objective knowledge, but it allows more for mystery, for being overturned into a new dimension that combines life and death in close proximity. Its impact will be like a sudden attack on the walls of certitude that have protected us; it may not be welcomed.

So much of preaching's usual presentation seems uncomfortable with Dionysus' gifts of intense feeling, emotion, intuition, and the incarnation of what Hillman calls "durable weakness and unheroic strength." When I listen to preaching, including my own, from an archetypal perspective I find most of us worship at Apollo's altar. So much of preaching is usually characterized by moderation, balance, clarity, a desire to appeal to reason, some mild effort to be imaginative (in a reasonable way), with some polite nods to literary aesthetics. Dionysus, however, is a very threatening god, and few may want to live in his turmoil for long. Yet he will rise up, suddenly, and overturn our static situations—now in this preacher, then in another. Listen for the reactions of "he's crazy" as was said of the carpenter's son so long ago. I think the spirit of Dionysus, which is one of the faces of the spirit of Jesus, is found more in the shaman than in the priest, for the former speaks out of his or her own religious experience and depths, whereas the role of the latter is to speak for the tradition. Yet, even though we might not dwell long or often in Dionysus, it is always possible to consider a Dionysian perspective when we approach a biblical text.

Preaching's Image as Dionysus

The Dionysian is found in those images that work to bring us to the depths, which is just where the sources of life are to be found. Dionysus is both the suffering god and the god of ecstasy and joy; he is the god of women and the god frequently imaged as a child, the god of liberation and the god of compassion for the least. If there is one gospel whose images seem to participate in and evoke this world more than any other, I would propose the gospel of Luke.

From the beginning there is a spirit of intoxication and ecstatic joy rooted in images of lives being overturned: the elderly Elizabeth and Zechariah, the young virgin Mary. Only in Luke do we have the image of a fetus leaping for joy in the womb. Joy burst forth in the songs of Zechariah, Mary and the angels chorusing out in a field to an audience of startled shepherds.

This note of joy sounded in the opening is sounded again at the conclusion of the gospel when Jesus ascends to heaven and the disciples "worshiped him, and returned to Jerusalem with great joy; and they were continually in the temple blessing God" (Lk 24:53).

More than any other gospel, Jesus' presence as a child is felt here, not only in the images of his conception and then his birth at Bethlehem, but also the scene of the presentation in the temple and the story about the young boy who stayed behind in the temple in Jerusalem while his parents frantically searched for him. His childhood also hinted at the suffering to come, particularly in the scene of the temple presentation when Simeon greets the child as one "destined for the falling and rising of many in Israel...a sign that will be opposed so that the inner thoughts of many will be revealed" (Lk 2:34-35). The resounding melody of joy is matched early on by chords of suffering.

From the beginning of his ministry, Jesus is presented as one who dissolves boundaries and provokes strong reactions. When he goes to his home synagogue to preach, the initially favorable reaction turns violent when he compares his ministry to Elijah and Elisha who both went beyond the boundaries of Israel. This Jesus is one who has come for all nations. Key to this dissolution of boundaries is the violent suffering that Jesus must undergo.

Luke's Jesus also dissolves the boundaries between men and women. Not only do the women have equally dominant roles in his infancy in such key figures as Mary, Elizabeth, and Anna, standing alongside Joseph, Zechariah, and Simeon. Luke presents us with the image of Jesus going through the towns and villages, preaching the gospel, accompanied not only by the twelve but also by some women he had cured, including Mary Magdalene, Joanna, Susanna, and many others who provided for them out of their resources (Lk 8:1-3). Luke presents Jesus' mother Mary as the ideal disciple, and his friend Mary, sister of Lazarus and Martha, as one sitting at his feet, the position of a disciple before a rabbi, unheard of for a woman.

Luke takes care to match male images with feminine images, for instance, when the widow of Zarephath is paired with Naaman the Syrian as figures of faith in Jesus' visit to Nazareth (Lk 4:25-27), or when he follows the parable of the shepherd finding the lost sheep with the woman finding the lost coin, offering here a female image of God (Lk 15:1-10). And Luke's Jesus even uses a female image for himself when he laments over Jerusalem and speaks of his desire to gather the children as a mother hen does her chicks (Lk 13:34). In Luke's Jesus we have a figure who is presented as the integration of traditionally masculine and feminine qualities, one who is filled with the driving power of the Spirit and an overflowing compassion for those in need.

This Jesus is one who forms and travels in community, welcoming not just women but all who are powerless. This is imaged not only in the incidents of his eating with sinners and tax collectors, but in the stories of Zacchaeus, the woman who comes in Simon the Pharisee's house to wash and anoint Jesus' feet, and the crucified thief who is promised paradise. All are also instances of dissolving boundaries. Jesus comes as one who liberates from the restrictions of the social and religious world of his day. He comes as a stranger and is often not welcomed, especially by power-brokers like Herod, Simon the Pharisee, and other members of the political and religious elite. But he comes impelled by the spirit that will overturn those who abuse power and status. Jesus comes bringing abundance of life, similar to that divinity who is shown surrounded by an abundance of vegetation, vines, and flowing wine.

While Luke's gospel often contains imagery that resonates with themes found in the Dionysian myth, any image in any of the biblical texts has the potential to function as Dionysus in presentation. Here are some questions that a preacher might ask when approaching an imaginal text with the goal of its functioning in the mode of Dionysus. I will use the imagery of the annunciation (Lk 1:26-38) as an example.

A) Can this imagery take a particular community at this time into contact with "the depths," where it can meet the forces of life and death, of dying and rising? How does this text pull us into a "madness" that can be the source of new creativity for this community? What darkness does it pull us toward? Has it any power to terrorize? Where in this text is the possibility of joy, ecstasy?

The central figures in the annunciation account are Mary and the angel, neither of whom at first glimpse would seem to open up "the depths." Could that be because we have domesticated this picture? Remember the first words of the angel, "Greetings, favored one. The Lord is with you." In this brief greeting, we are given a glimpse into the depths of a theological vision. Mary is the graced one, the favored one. She is one with whom God is present. In this greeting given to the one whom Luke presents as the ideal disciple is the basis for dying and rising, for joy and ecstasy.

B) How does this text dismember and loosen this community from social constructs that constrain and stifle? What conventions does it overturn? How does it offer liberation and freedom in a way that can overturn and usher in a new kingdom? Mary Catherine Hilkert writes that "many personal and social issues that touch women daily are rarely or inadequately addressed from the pulpit. These issues include sexism, racism, violence against women, and abuse against children. Women's voices need to be heard on these issues."[14] One needs to ask: How does this text champion women? How does it confront a world of masculine power, prestige, and privilege?

Again, this text calls us to loosen ourselves from how we may have heard this text in past renderings. Mary is often presented as the passive, demure little maiden. This is possibly due to her initial reaction of being "perplexed by his words and pondering what sort of greeting this might be," and Gabriel's subsequent response, "Do not be afraid, Mary...." But when one considers the image as a whole, we have a young woman who from the start is presented as thoughtful (she ponders, considers what has just been said to her), questioning (her "how

can this be since I do not know man?" could not be more to the point),
and decisive ("Here am I, the servant of the Lord; let it be with me
according to your word"). She then acts, going off to visit and give
assistance to her cousin Elizabeth.

Such a presentation presents an image of women's role in God's saving work in a manner that can certainly confront some of the more
patriarchal attitudes that still seem in the ascendancy both in society and
in the church. Furthermore, in Mary as the ideal disciple we have a
model of an adult relationship with God that encourages thoughtfulness,
questioning, decision-making, and assertive action.

C) How does this text help directly or indirectly to integrate the
realm of the repressed? How does it link us with the earth, with the
body, with the female and male in all of us, with the soul?

This text presents the image of the flesh as something most sacred,
as the home of divinity, *if* consent be given. Further-more, the earth is
seen as the locus for the long-range plan of God's salvation, stretching
backward to the origin of all life and forward into the end time. Mary is
to be imitated by all disciples, men and women; she is the prototype of
discipleship.

D) Can this imagery offer the possibility of transformation? From
what to what? Does it allow for any epiphany, any sudden revelation?
Can this text help to transform social structures in which we have
grown comfortable but which are increasingly lifeless, perhaps even
death-dealing?

With the 1993 Christmas issue of *Time* magazine proclaiming that
almost 60% of Americans say they believe in angels, and the most
recent Pulitzer prize winning play, *Angels in America*, featuring one
angel in the lead and several others in the wings, this imaginal account
of an invitation to bring divinity into the world would seem to invite
faith in a transformation by a greater power that overshadows. It also
reminds us that epiphany often occurs right at home.

I would like to conclude by offering an example of a homily that
attempts to work in the Dionysian mode. Using this text of the annunciation, I preached on the feast of the Immaculate Conception, a
Roman Catholic feast that celebrates Mary's being graced from the
first moment of her existence in view of the saving death of Jesus that
won salvation for all. Mary is not usually seen as a figure that can

overturn the world. Most women's experience of her might correspond more to novelist Mary Gordon's reflections on growing up with Mary:

> In my day, Mary was a stick to beat smart girls with. Her example was held up constantly: an example of silence, of subordination, of the pleasure of taking the back seat. With the kind of smile they would give to the behavior of Margaret the wife in "Father Knows Best," they talked about the one assertion of Mary's recorded in the gospel: her request at the wedding feast at Cana. It was noted that she didn't ask her son directly for anything; she merely said: "They have no more wine." Making him think it was his decision. Not suggesting it was her idea, no, nothing like that. Then disappearing, once again into the background, into silence.[15]

Gordon goes on to say that for any hope of intellectual achievement, independence of identity, or sexual fulfillment it was necessary to reject images such as these. For her the loss of Mary was the loss of a powerful female image whose appeal and application were universal. Gordon herself managed to retrieve this image for her own soul, but some women still repudiate Mary as a male re-creation of what a woman should be.[16]

The feast of the Immaculate Conception, with its emphasis on Mary's sinlessness, can remove Mary even further from the possibility of human identification. However, by attending to its imaginal texts (Genesis 3:9-15.20, Ephesians 1:3-6.11-12, and Luke 1:26-38) a preacher can find an opportunity to place before the community an imaginal world capable of subverting the distance and present Mary as a model for choice and God as One who from the beginning surrounds all of us with love.

A Tale of Two Sisters

When Romeo first sees Juliet,
he is overcome by beauty:
"O she doth teach the torches to burn bright.
It seems she hangs upon the cheek of night

As a rich jewel in an Ethiop's ear;
Beauty too rich for use, for earth too dear."

The church has often had a similar response to Mary.
She released the poetry in an often prose-filled soul.
"Mystical rose," we cried.
"Tower of ivory, House of gold, Ark of the covenant."
Over the years, like Juliet,
Mary became perched up there somewhere.
On a pedestal, if not a balcony.
And today's feast can reinforce her distance from us.
"You kept her sinless from the first moment of her conception,"
we acknowledge in the opening prayer.

Must we, Romeo-like, only stand stunned before this mystery.
Distantly appreciative,
separated by an uncrossable gap.
Or is what seems an overgrown divide possibly a bridge,
covered over by vines and weeds,
but, like the secret garden, able to be uncovered.

On this feast,
a diptych is set before us.
First, Mother Eve.
In the garden, fruit juice running down her chin.
Perhaps a piece of the fruit's skin stuck in her teeth.
To my mind, it had to be an apple.
A pear isn't sufficiently sensuous.
An orange's skin is too thick, certainly not a lemon.
Plums grow up to be prunes and a banana is too Freudian.
So, a bright, red, sweet, luscious apple.
I used to think once she bit into it, she found it mealy!
But God isn't a sadist, is she?

To have so much hang on a piece of fruit.
But that's often the case in the most important tales.
The pricking from a spinning wheel for Sleeping Beauty.
A glass slipper for Cinderella, a gold key for Iron John.

But let us not be diverted.
A piece of fruit was nibbled,
A choice was made.
The woman *and* the man made it.
And in choosing the fruit, a world was unmade,
an opportunity rejected.
Good word—opportunity—from the Latin, *porta*, for gate.
The gate was closed behind us.
And an angel with a flaming sword barred the way back.
Another world began—
conceived in rebellion—"No" being the battle cry—
and nurtured in blame—
"the woman made me do it…"
"the serpent made me do it."
More than one gate slammed shut.
Trust had closed over on several fronts.
That is the first frame of our diptych.

In the second frame
we find a young woman who could be her sister.

It is the first image Luke gives us of Mary.
In many paintings of the Annunciation
she is portrayed in something that looks like the house
chapel, kneeling at a priedieu.
One stained glass window I've seen even has
what appears to be a confessional in the background!
I rather think of her as being out in the garden,
a parallel to our first image,
Tending the flowers and the vegetables, some vines,
a fruit tree in the background.

We come upon her looking up at someone,
a figure, standing, with the sun behind, face in the shadow,
a halo effect surrounding the head.
A greeting: "Rejoice, highly favored daughter,
        full of grace,
        the Lord is with you…blessed are you.…"

She feels an inner dread, as though she's seen her own death.
Then, again the figure speaks:
    "Don't be afraid...
    you have found favor with God;
    you will conceive and bear a son
    and he will be called Son of the Most High
    and you will name him Jesus...."
Mary's response is direct,
    "How is this supposed to happen?
    I haven't slept with any man."
Not the demure little princess,
but a practical young woman.

Then the words of promise:
    "The Holy Spirit will come upon you
    and the power of the most High overshadow you...
    the one born will be called Son of God."

Silence invades the space; she can barely breathe.
In many pictures, Mary's eyes are downcast, looking inward.
Native Americans honor four kinds of sight:
    the vision of the buffalo which sees both foreground and
    background,
    the vision of the field mouse which can see close-up,
    the vision of the eagle which is panoramic,
    and the vision of the hibernating bear which looks within.
This image of Mary with downcast eyes captures this inner vision.
In the pause before pregnancy, Mary looks within
and sees there the image of God she already carries.
Before she bore him in her womb, she bore him in her heart,
Augustine tells us.
In looking in, she sees the landscape of grace,
she feels the presence of God.
Suddenly, she says, "Yes"
And a gate swings open.
Opportunity accepted.

Eve and Mary, our sisters.
Their stories are ours.
They stand before us
     in their gardens
     and remind us:
In the beginning,
     every beginning,
     God.
God, the Loving Mother who gave us the garden of life
     and every day calls us to tend this garden,
      with its new possibilities.
Mother Wisdom that designed the hills and the mountains,
      that called forth the plants and the animals,
      and that fashioned man and woman in her image.

In the beginning, a choice, an opportunity,
      a gate to be opened that offers entry into divinity,
      that we be holy and blameless in her sight,
      that we be full of love.
And the gift of a choice: yes or no.

In the beginning, the gift of freedom:
     if we say No,
     Eden's gate slams shut once again
     and the world knows a deeper darkness because of us;
     if we say Yes,
     God takes flesh, ours, and God is incarnated
     and the earth blossoms
     and we take part in the great song:
Our soul magnifies the Lord
and our spirit gives joy to God, our Savior.
And God is born again and again in holy flesh
in the power of spirit.

The call of Dionysus is to dissolve the familiar and enter into a realm
in which life and death are intertwined. The preaching that comes from
this realm calls for change, for conversion of heart, a radical turning
from one direction toward another. Images that lead the community

toward a fullness of life by dying and rising, to a deeper freedom, to a fuller integration of humanity in both men and women, and transformative and epiphanic experiences of joy and ecstasy—such belong to the archetypal experience of Dionysus. But we must not forget the darker side of this divinity with its potential for violence, terror, upheaval, and madness that also characterize this archetypal world. For it is by such consciousness that we might better understand how other images have such destructive power.

The direction of Dionysus is often represented as downward, into the depths, in contrast to Apollo's ascent into the heights. Both are important movements for the soul. There remains still one other movement to be considered here, that constellated by the figure of the god Hermes, the guide who moves us *through*.

6.
Imaginal Preaching and Hermes

"Hermes: thief...
...carrier of dreams...
messenger of the gods...
guide,
giver of good things..."
(Homeric Hymns to Hermes)

An Experience of Hermes

In this final reflection on archetypal presences in imagery, I would like to relate how an image came to offer movement and meaning for my soul. Meaning and movement belong in a special way to Hermes, the messenger god and the god of the journey. Hermes is also associated with change and places of change; therefore, the marketplace, the place of intersecting roads, and the arcane process of alchemy belong to him. But our particular concern is how the soul moves when meaning shifts. To exemplify, a story.

For nearly half a century I lived under the gaze of an icon. It was present in my home as a child and has been in almost every home and many of the churches in which I have spent any substantial time. This particular icon honored Mary, the mother of Jesus, under the title "Our Mother of Perpetual Help." While it had the aloof beauty that is characteristic of most icons, for most of my life it functioned more as a

Hermes.

blocked entry than a "window on eternity." I had an uncomfortable feeling every time I looked at it, finding it cold and unapproachable.

The icon portrays the mother of Jesus, holding her son, here presented not as an infant but as a young boy. On either side of the mother and
child is an angel, one carrying the cross and nails, and the other, a lance
and sponge. The child is looking at one of the angels, but the mother is
gazing outward, directly into the eyes of the viewer. The child's left foot
has a sandal dangling from its ankle, barely held by a thin strap. As a
child I was told a story that explained the events leading up to this
moment. One day Jesus was playing outside when two angels appeared
before him, bearing the instruments of his passion and death. Becoming
frightened, he ran into the house and leapt into his mother's arms with
such force that his one sandal came loose. She holds him close as his
hands clasp her right hand. The image's presentation of Mary as one
who protects and comforts was easily extended to all who turn to her in
prayer, hence the title "*Our* Mother of Perpetual Help."

Only a few years ago did I realize why I had never had much affec-
tion for this icon. One day I was gazing at a small reproduction and, out
of the blue, I recalled a voice from long ago, saying, "See how the sandal
dangles from Jesus' foot. He was so frightened by the angels that he
jumped into Mary's arms, almost losing his sandal. And look at his
mother. She is looking at each one here with great sorrow, asking, 'Will
you also hurt my son by your sins?'" I don't know whose voice it was
that first said these words; time has disembodied it and rendered it face-
less. But that voice and the interpretation it offered framed my experience of the icon for over forty years. Its title may have been "Our
Mother of Perpetual Help" but its effect on me more accurately rendered
it "Our Mother of Perpetual Guilt." I could never look at it without feeling some twinge of guilt for past, present, or even future transgressions.

But a change happened with that recovered memory. The image had
become loosened from its frame. This serendipitous experience of
remembering that voice proved to be a grace, because I could finally lift
off the frame these words had created and allow the image to function
free of this single constricting interpretation. Movement and fluidity
were restored both to the image and my interaction with it. *New* meanings were possible.

From an archetypal perspective, such an experience can be laid at the feet of Hermes. The sudden gift of an image that brings new meaning and allows new movement can be linked with the archetypal figure that moves us along through the obstacles and seeming opacity of life. If Apollo speaks to us of image's power to bring stability and order into our world, and Dionysus of image's ability to violently rend the stable world asunder, Hermes' presence in imagery playfully subverts everything that stops the flow, inhibits motion, and impedes our journey *through* the world. Not ascent or descent but movement *through* is most pertinent to Hermes' world. Let us consider some of his images.

Hermes' World

a. *Hermes, Trickster and Thief.* Born of Zeus and the nymph Maia, Hermes establishes his identity from the first hours of his life. By the end of the first day, he had not only stolen away from his mother, but he had stolen the herd of cows belonging to Apollo, his elder half-brother. As he was leading the cows away from their pasture, he noticed their tracks; so he turned their back hooves frontward and their front hooves backward, reversing their tracks, and he himself walked backward. Thus, his first attempt at playing the trickster. Hermes is a thief, not a robber; he resorts to trickery and stealth rather than force. When Apollo eventually appeared at the door of his home, Maia pointed to her infant son, who had successfully slipped back into his cradle and was feigning sleep, and she protested the innocence of such a small innocent babe. Apollo was not fooled but snatched the child, calling him "Prince of Thieves," and took him to Olympus to answer to their father, Zeus.

b. *Hermes, Messenger of the Gods.* When Apollo stood with his younger brother before Zeus, Hermes swore to his innocence, lying so smoothly that Zeus finally exploded in laughter. Cutting short Hermes' eloquent defense, Zeus sternly warned his son that another's property should be respected and he must stop telling lies. Then Zeus added, "You seem to be a very ingenious, eloquent, and persuasive godling!" Hermes responded, "Then, make me your herald, Father, and I will never tell lies, though I cannot promise always to tell the whole truth!" In this way, Hermes came to be the messenger of the gods and goddesses, and his father Zeus gave him the winged staff, called the caduceus, the winged hat, and the winged sandals. These items are found in art works like Giambologna's Hermes, which shows the messenger captured in mid-flight. Hermes is constantly on the go and is marked by an attentiveness to any opening, no matter how small, easily moving through it, blurring any boundaries that separate.

Hermes' response to Zeus also bears special notice. The infant god says that, while he won't tell any lies, he can't promise always to tell the whole truth. Plato did not go far enough when he said Hermes was the inventor of language and speech since he gave mortals the alphabet. More to the point is Hermes' link with eloquence, with "winged words," and the "twisted truth" of metaphor. He is also the god of night and of night's language, dreams, bringing them across the borders of our consciousness. One of his names is "the Whisperer."

c. *Hermes, God of the Windfall.* Unexpected luck, surprises, and sudden finds are attributed to Hermes. On his first day of life, he came across a tortoise outside his door and seized it. Laughing, he called this timid, introverted creature, "companion of the festival"; then, he took it inside, killed it, and used its shell to fashion a lyre, fulfilling the promise he had sensed in it. This incident captures Hermes' ability to see through what is before him and to recognize surprising possibilities. He brings with him the gift of insight into the concreteness of life and the ability to perceive the hidden possibilities of what lies beneath the surface.

Windfall was the name given to the food offerings that were left at roadside herms, those phallus-shaped stone pillars representing the god of the crossroads. In the spirit of Hermes, hungry travelers were encouraged to "steal" the offerings so they could continue the journey. These same stone herms, being so permanent and unmovable, offer a paradoxical note to the image of Hermes. The usual image of energy in motion is balanced by the immobility of stone. But the line between matter and energy is more flexible than our senses tell us, signaling Hermes' ability to cross such boundaries.

d. *Hermes the Guide.* When Hector, prince of Troy, lay dead behind the enemy lines of the Greeks and the great Achilles refused to give Hector's body to his father, King Priam, Hermes came to the rescue. He guided the old man past the soldiers, putting them to sleep with his magical staff. In this way, Priam was able to recover his son's corpse and see to its burial. By being able to bury his son, Priam's soul could begin to move beyond that tragic loss. Hermes was the guide for all travelers and was said to be the friendliest of all the gods; he was called "the god who draws near" and was to be found at the crossroads and turning points, those places where one world intersects with another. He also guided souls to the underworld, most notably the suitors of Penelope whom Odysseus had killed, and each year he guided Persephone back to earth, after she had spent the winter with Hades. As the guide of souls, he is called the Psychopomp, linking him with all who offer direction to the soul. He is the god of the journey, the voyage, the adventure; his preference is for the winding path rather than the straight road. Always on the go, Hermes is often pictured as darting, running, moving by leaps and bounds.

e. *Hermes the Rescuer.* In one version of Dionysus' birth, Hermes, rather than Zeus, seized the unborn god from the womb of his mother Semele just as she was about to be consumed by Zeus' thunderbolts and then sewed him into his father's thigh. In the Olympia museum is a marble statue by Praxiteles, showing Hermes carrying the infant Dionysus to the nymphs who were to bring him up. And in the *Iliad*, Hermes appeared to Odysseus and gave him the gift of moly, a black rooted herb with a beautiful white flower, to protect him from the bewitchment of the enchantress, Circe, who had turned Odysseus' men into swine. Taking on the appearance of a ram, Hermes rescued young Phrixus, son of King Athamus, just as his father's sacrificial knife was about to sink into the boy's flesh. And he saved the lovely Io from the hundred-eyed Argus by alternately singing and playing his pipe in such a boring way that all the creature's eyes eventually fell asleep. Hermes as rescuer saves what is innocent, vulnerable, sacred—or, in the case of Odysseus, a fellow trickster like himself.

In summary, Hermes is most important for facilitating movement, whether of the body, the mind, or the soul. He is the eloquent messenger who speaks in the deviant discourse of metaphor, the twisted truth. Hermes is the god of everyday reality who points to the world of meaning beneath the surface of things, moving us forward, keeping the journey going, discovering new openings and deciding on new paths at the crossroads, preferring those that wind and twist through the countryside. To him also belongs delight, spontaneity, laughter, cleverness, wonder, fluidity, and play. All are helpful qualities for those on a journey where flexibility is important to meet a sudden need for change. He was called Mercurius by the Romans because of his ability to quickly transform himself; he is also the patron of alchemy, the art by which base metals are changed into gold. Above all, Hermes embodies the power of moving through and crossing over.

Hermes' World, the Preacher's World

Hermes' world is entered by those who participate in the work of the guide and messenger, the trickster and thief, the traveler and companion, the whisperer of night and day dreams—in particular by those preachers who recognize the ability of language to move and guide, play and transform those who are "on the way." Hermes meets us at the crossroads and transitional points of life and beckons us to cross boundaries. Of the three archetypal figures considered in this second half of the book, I most enjoy entertaining the presence of Hermes in thought and imagination. He is the guiding soul-image for the work of preaching in the everyday. While I can appreciate the need for the heights of Apollo and the gifts of clarity, precision, far sightedness that he signals, and while I can recognize the need for Dionysus' power for disruption, overturning certainties that have ceased to be life-giving, evoking a way of being and faithful response that is rooted in risk more than obedience, it is the imaginal presence and archetypal power of Hermes that encourages me to keep on going. The reality of being part of a pilgrim people, always straining to exodus from slavery to freedom, allows me to entertain this mythic presence.

One artist who works in words to create a world where Hermes moves is the South African playwright, Athol Fugard. Fugard's people offer one another and us images that provoke inner movement of the soul. I believe his language also has had the power to move those who hear his message to change the world around them. While most of his work directly confronts the world of apartheid, he also has provided one of the most moving plays about the role of the artist in society.

In *The Road to Mecca*, Fugard presents Miss Helen, an elderly Afrikaner widow living in the arid region of the Karoo, who is at a crossroads in her life. Due to a growing inability to care for herself, her old friend and pastor of the local church, Marius Byleveld, is strongly pressuring her to go into a church–sponsored home for the elderly. However, her young English friend, Elsa Barlow, a teacher from Cape Town, sees this as an attempt to take away Miss Helen's freedom. For

Elsa, Miss Helen is the embodiment of self-liberation, a person who has freed herself from the narrow world of her small town and its conservative values, through her choice of a life of artistic expression. Responding to Miss Helen's call for support, Elsa has driven all night to be with Helen and strengthen her resolve to stay where she is. When Marius comes by to have Helen sign the papers for living at the home, the battle lines have been clearly drawn for the trophy of Miss Helen's soul.

The power of the play rests on Miss Helen's witness to a guiding power that has been with her for some time. Her arrival at the present crossroads is the result of having successfully navigated some earlier ones. She speaks of the night of her husband's funeral more than a decade earlier, after all had left her in her home. With eloquent simplicity she tells how the only light in the room was a candle which eventually went out, or *seemed* to, for, suddenly, it began to "find its courage again. It started to get brighter and brighter. I didn't know whether I was awake any longer or dreaming because a strange feeling came over me...that it was leading me...leading me far away to a place I had never been to before."[1] A sense of guidance, leading onward, is the mark of Hermes.

And Miss Helen followed. The decisive moment came one Sunday morning, shortly after that evening. An image came to her during the night. "I just had to go to work immediately while it was still fresh in my mind." And with that decision, Miss Helen first crossed the boundary that separated her from all she had known and went into uncharted land. An image carried her across. At that moment image functioned as Hermes, leading her in a new direction. Miss Helen witnesses to its power, reminding Marius that her decision was not an easy one:

> But don't ever think that missing church that Sunday was something I did lightly, Marius. You don't break the habit of a lifetime without realizing that life will never quite be the same again. I was already dressed and ready! I had my Bible and hymnbook, I was on the point of leaving this room as I had done every Sunday for as long as I could remember...but I knew that if It did, I would never make that owl....[2]

And so Miss Helen began to carve statues in her yard, figures of mermaids, camels, wise men, owls and other mythic creatures.

All this, along with Helen's increasing isolation, has been an affront to Helen's old neighbors and friends, an embarrassment to the community. Furthermore, recently Helen accidentally started a fire that almost burned the house down. So, Marius' concern is operating on several levels—as friend, pastor, and custodian of the community's values. Finally, hurt and angry, he accuses her of turning her back on her church, her faith, her friends, and himself, asking, "For what? For those statues out there that can't give you love or take care of you the way we wanted to?" Miss Helen answers him in a way that again places us in the realm of Hermes, this time as the god of language and eloquence. For her, a new language was necessary; the old one had failed.

> ...I tried hard, Marius, but your sermons, the prayers, the hymns, they had all become just words. And there came a time when even they lost their meaning.
>
> Do you know what the word "God" looks like when you've lost your faith? It looks like a little stone, a cold, round, little stone. "Heaven" is another one, but it's got an awkward useless shape, while "Hell" is flat and smooth. All of them—damnation, grace, salvation—a handful of stones.[3]

Miss Helen left that "handful of stones" and exchanged them for her own garden of carved statues: owls, wise men, buddhas and mermaids. In a sense one handful of stones was exchanged for another; but where there had been no life, there was now abundance.

From words that are dead stones to stones that are a living language, a road to Mecca that begins in a South African garden. Language, movement, a dream that initiates a journey, playful figures of mermaids, wise men, camels, an alchemical transformation of the soul, one friend stolen, another given—all these images point in a particular archetypal direction. Fugard's work here also speaks of a fourth character present in this ostensibly three character play—Hermes, Psychopomp, leader of souls, taking Miss Helen across one boundary after another. Fugard's other plays are also full of movement, physical and psychological, literal and metaphorical, and, in the final analysis, spiritual, providing images that function in a Hermetic mode not only

for his characters but for all who listen. Perhaps Miss Helen is his figure for the artist, who gives expression to the soul of the nation, and
must keep going on alone into new places. Later in this chapter I shall
draw on some of the images from another Fugard play used in a homily for a baptism.

When I, as a preacher, am in Hermes' world, I have a different kind
of outlook than at other times. I am concerned with facilitating movement so that my community might continue their journey, whether it is
seen as slouching toward Bethlehem to be born anew, or hastening
toward Jerusalem to walk the way to Golgotha, or moving from a place
of tears to a serendipitous meeting on the road to Emmaus. Hermetic
awareness is a movement that attends to the importance of being in
what is called "the between." Hillman is helpful when he speaks of
imagining "Hermetic awareness less as a transcendent function that
holds the opposites together, or overcomes them, and more as a consciousness that *requires and even creates a betweenness in which to
operate*."[4] This realm of the "between" can vary in its two poles:
between life and death, between present and future, between dream and
daylight, between the world of the congregation and the world of the
Bible, and between faith and unbelief—to name a few possibilities.

Such a "between" space provides ground on which one can stand
and search for relationships between "x" and "y," becoming attentive to
parallels, analogies, likenesses, and family resemblances that are there
to be discovered between one reality and another. This is why the
"between" gives birth to metaphorical expression. Metaphorical consciousness is Hermetic consciousness. From the "between" comes
knowledge of how one thing *is* and *is not* something else. The
"between" as a metaphorical space and a space for creating metaphor
thereby serves as a playground. Whether discovering new metaphors or
breathing new life into old ones, the preacher plays with words, ideas,
sacred mysteries, and sacred rituals.

Hermes calls the preacher to be playful, to participate in the role of
the trickster, surprising listeners with sudden discoveries of things pre-
viously unseen or sudden thefts of long held perspectives. When anthro-
pologist Victor Turner speaks of ritual as liminality, he notes that there
are three components: the communication of the *sacra*, that is, the
sacred stories, words, things, actions; acts of *ludic recombination*, a

type of playing with cultural traits in a way that subverts them and results in new perceptions on life; and, finally, the creation of what is called *communitas*, a condition in which all participants are undifferentiated by rank, status, or other qualities that create inequality.[5]

Turner's three components can be seen as applicable to most liturgical rituals, particularly the celebration of the eucharist. I would propose that the ludic recombination takes place especially in the preaching, when the preacher makes use of the sacred texts to subvert cultural traits and perspectives through the challenge of the gospel. The communication of the *sacra* that takes place in the reading of the scripture leads into a playful use of biblical text interacting with the text of life, which in turn leads into a state of *communitas* in which all know themselves to be of equal worth before God. Notice that the work of ludic recombination falls in the middle position, in the "between." Without it, the movement from the sharing of the *sacra* to a condition of true communion will not occur. It can only happen if there is some degree of "play," the central characteristic of liminality.[6]

The playful Hermetic preacher is unafraid to evoke laughter, knowing the role of the clown is as effective as the solemnity of the Apollonian prophet or the terror of the Dionysian mystic in the preaching task. The sound of laughter in church can be the signal that starts a community's soul moving once again. Unfortunately, sometimes we do not recognize or we refuse the invitations to play that can be found in the scriptures. These can come both in the way that a preacher interprets the text when reading it to the community and in the way a text is entertained (a word that means "to hold in the between") in the preaching moment.

I can remember seeing the performance of the gospel of St. Mark by the actor Alec McCowen. His masterful interpretation managed to bring out the humor that was in the text. One instance was his portrayal of a very tired Jesus and an equally tired apostle bickering over feeding the crowd of five thousand. "Shouldn't they be sent away?" begins the apostle. "Give them something to eat," Jesus retorts. Then, with accelerating heat, "And where are we to get the money?" "Go and see how many loaves there are." "Five…(long pause, then in exasperation) and two fish." McCowen managed to convey the testiness in both parties in a way that evoked smiles of recognition, and a segment often solemnized into stolidity suddenly came to life. He made us see a very human Jesus, worn down by exhaustion and the dull-headedness of his own disciples, while bringing out the humor in the scene. The rapid exchange of comments could be appreciated by anyone who has spoken through gritted teeth, clamped down as much due to exhaustion as anger. The effect of such playfulness with the text was to make Jesus a more accessible figure solely through the vocal interpretation of Mark's words.

Play can also be found helpful while preparing to preach. Play with the words that carry the stories, images, and ideas. I find the author Frederick Buechner another model of Hermes' playfulness, whether dealing with biblical characters or biblical ideas, sending our imaginations off in new directions. For Buechner, the mystery of the incarnation means that "all ground is holy ground because God not only made it but walked on it, ate and slept and worked and died on it"; a Christian is one "who is on the way, though not necessarily very far along it, and who has at least some dim and half-baked idea of whom to thank"; and true repentance "spends less time looking at the past and saying, 'I'm sorry,' than to the future and saying 'Wow!'"[7]

Buechner gives delight with his insight into characters that we have heard about again and again over the years. He has the facility to offer us a phrase that allows us to look at them in a fresh way as unexpected companions for our own journey. He gives us a post-Eden Eve, waking up from beautiful and sad dreams, "homesick for a home she could no longer even name, to make something not quite love with a man whose face she could not quite see in the darkness at her side"; Joseph's brothers, "seething at the sight of the many colored coat he flaunted while they were running around in T-shirts and dirty jeans"; mission-battered Paul, "punch-drunk and Christ-drunk," and guilt-stricken Peter with "tears running down his face like rain down a rock." There is even an imaginary scene between Christ and Judas after their deaths, based on an early church tradition of Judas committing suicide out of hope rather than despair: "Once again they met in the shadows, the two old friends, both of them a little worse for wear after all that had happened, only this time it was Jesus who was the one to give the kiss, and this time it wasn't the kiss of death that was given."[8]

Buechner's work opens new ways for us to enter the biblical world and the lives of its people. He finds openings in the walls that divide our own age from the mythic past of our ancestors in the faith, some-times allowing us to slip through and see life from where they stood, at other times permitting them to slip into our world and take on our cyni-cism and inability to look beyond the visible to things unseen.

Playing with the sacred stories and with the texts of our own lives can crack open what has become a sealed enclosure. Throughout the Judaeo-Christian tradition the great stories have been told and retold in a way that constantly reinterprets them. This is what keeps them alive. The danger is that even our sacred stories have become what one of Amanda Cross' characters called a "potted narrative," that is, "a story, like the story of the birth of my children, readily available as anecdote because I have got it pat. What I tell of course is not the past but the story I have made of the past, which encloses it and saves me from rein-terpretation."[9] Hermes, the god whose name is contained in the task of hermeneutics, calls us to interpret and reinterpret the tales we have received. When we let them harden, they lose their inner life and the capacity to stir up life in us. Preachers must unpot the narratives, replanting them in a setting appropriate to where life is being lived now, allowing the roots contained in the biblical imagery and narratives to stretch and expand, facilitating further growth—ours!

The preacher who approaches the preaching task from the archetypal perspective of Hermes can be seen as enabling transformation by serv-ing as a bridge which facilitates movement from one place to another. Stassinopoulos writes that Hermes is a "bridge between ourselves and what we feel greater than ourselves, between what we know and what we dimly perceive, what we are and are not and yet feel called upon to become, between the last horizon of our known self and the compelling mystery which encloses it as the universe the earth."[10] Hermes' transfor-mation is different than that of Dionysus. The latter's is sudden and often disruptive, whereas Hermes offers a more gradual transformation, as he circuitously guides us through what lies ahead.

Preaching's Image as Hermes

Hermes' power and presence are found in the images of our tradition when they function according to the pattern of his archetypal world of whispering messages, guiding metaphors, and horizontal movement. The shadow of Hermes can be glimpsed especially in the gospel of

Mark's presentation of Jesus, and in the themes that receive special prominence there. As Apollo has been linked with Matthew and Dionysus with Luke, it is serendipitously appropriate to play with Hermes' relationship to the first of the synoptics.

Hermes' spirit is imaged in the Jesus of the journey, the Messiah on the move, crossing boundaries that transcend the geographical lines separating Judea, Samaria, and Galilee. Jesus moves freely across the divide between Jews and Gentiles, men and women, rich and poor, saved and sinner. He is the one who is presented as being in opposition to those who are immovable. Jesus moves easily not only through the geographical terrain but also the social and religious landscape. When told that everyone in Capernaum is looking for him to continue his preaching and healing, he replies, "Let us go on to the neighboring towns, so that I may proclaim the message there also; for that is what I came out to do" (Mk 1:38).

Mark's Jesus is the messenger. Some contemporary scholarship even argues that the opening quote from Isaiah referring to the messenger sent ahead who will prepare your way (Mk 1:2-3) refers not to John the Baptist but to Jesus.[11] Mark presents Jesus' first act of ministry as fulfilling the role of message-bearer: "The time is fulfilled and the kingdom of God has come near; repent and believe in the good news" (Mk 1:15). The oldest gospel presents Jesus as the eloquent one who speaks in metaphors and parables: of a sower and scattered seeds, of seed growing according to its own laws, of mustard seeds being transformed into the greatest of all shrubs, and of wicked tenant farmers whose lives bear the poisonous fruit of violence and murder. He uses words in a way that creates twisting paths for his hearers, leading them where they might not wish to go—more deeply into the encounter with the God revealed in the very being of the messenger. Hermes' designation as the whisperer also has a resonance with Mark's Jesus, who explains to his disciples in secret the meaning of the parables and whispers to them the messianic secret regarding his identity as one who will suffer and die.

Like Hermes, Jesus is one who rescues the child, seen in his healing of children such as the daughters of Jairus and of the Syrophoenician woman and the boy possessed by an evil spirit. He also is one who both holds children in his embrace and holds them up as worthy of imitation. In a world where children were viewed as having no value, as being little more than property, Jesus takes them in his arms, lays his hands on them, and blesses them. The child is presented as the inheritor of the kingdom; the disciples are not only chided when they try to prevent children from coming to Jesus, but, when they are engaged in arguing over who was the greatest, he places a child before them. For Jesus and his followers, the child is a figure of trusting faith, of openness to the coming kingdom. Jesus gives one of his strongest rebukes when he notes that it were better to have a millstone tied around your neck than to lead a little one astray. And he makes one of his strongest statements of a child's value when he says that "Whoever welcomes one such child in my name welcomes me and whoever welcomes me welcomes the one who sent me" (Mk 9:37).

Finally, Jesus is the psychopomp, the guide of souls, leading them to mountains, shorelines, and places set apart. He guides those who follow him through life, calling them to choose to live a life of faith rather than fear, to live for others rather than for oneself. He invites all to join him in the journey from anxiety to courage. Jesus is the faithful guide to disciples, choosing them, empowering them to preach and heal, and, despite their hardheadedness and hardheartedness, remaining faithful to them even in the face of their final desertion, denial, and betrayal. The young man sitting on the right side of the empty tomb tries to calm the fears of the women, telling them to give Jesus' message of implicit reconciliation to Peter and the disciples, guiding them back to Galilee.

That same message is given to every reader of Mark's gospel. When the final silence of death seems to settle over the story of Jesus, a note of hope is sounded. In the Easter message, all of us are invited to return to Galilee, to meet Jesus there, and to walk again with him through the gospel story. Jesus is the one who enables all his disciples to keep moving toward the final end, to that hour when they shall see the Son of Man coming on the clouds.

The various aspects of the archetypal world of Hermes, the particular qualities that constellate the Hermetic pattern, can be considered in approaching any imaginal text. Let us consider one last time some of the questions with which a preacher can approach any imaginal text, facilitating that image's ability to function in the manner of Hermes within the consciousness of a community. We will use Mark's account of Jesus' baptism (Mk 1:9-11) as a focus for our questions.

A. How do the text's images help a community to move onward, to navigate a particular crossroads? Here, the image of Jesus in the Jordan is one of heaven and earth intersecting: the Nazarene Jesus coming up out of the water as the heavens are "torn asunder," and the Spirit descends. Jesus himself is presented as the crosspoint between heaven and earth; moreover, he is presented as *the* transitional figure of all history, about to start on his journey of mission.

The image of Jesus' baptism imaginally interprets for a community gathered for baptism what is happening to their children. It provides a way of thinking about the particular transitional moment in which they are presently involved. They stand with their child at a crossroads and have decided to set out on a journey with the Lord. This day through the preacher they can understand themselves to stand in the flowing Jordan with their child and witness the heavens being torn open and the spirit descending.

B. How does this text through its images convey a message for this community? How is this imaginal text a messenger? What is it "saying" to us in its imagery? There is Jesus coming out of water that reminds us of the waters of chaos at the time of creation, the waters of the flood, the waters that swept over the threatening Egyptians who would prevent the exodus to freedom. Here the words addressed only to Jesus can be overheard by the community present as addressed to their children: "*You* are my beloved, my chosen; on *you* my favor rests." What God whispers to Jesus is being whispered to these little ones. And then the eloquent image of the heavens being torn asunder, a dove descending.

C. What guidance does this image offer? The Spirit that comes upon Jesus in this event drives him first into the desert, then into the long road of his ministry. In a similar fashion, the community is reminded that the Spirit that comes upon these children will be with them in the times both of the desert and of the life journey that stretches before them. This past week has brought news of an earthquake in India that has taken the lives of over 21,000 people, of an open shooting in southeast Washington, D.C. during a pick-up football game that not only took the life of a twenty-one year old black man but also a four year old black girl, of a Korean woman murdered in her store in northeast Washington, D.C. This text guides us in a world where such events occur, reminding all of the relationship of parent to child that names how we stand before our God, and that we have been gifted with the Spirit. From the conscious appropriation of such images, behavior flows.

D. How does this text allow the community to engage in play that leads us to ponder the truth of life? What cultural traits can this text address, reinforce, contradict, subvert? How does this text invite us into what Turner calls "ludic recombination," the analysis of and toying with cultural traits, which has as its goal to draw those present to ponder values, attitudes, behavior? How does this text move the community to think freshly about people, objects, relationships, social roles, the environment?

Hermes creates a "between" in which to move back and forth. Consider this text as a between space, between the everyday world in which we now move and the world to which we are heading, between the past events that happened to Jesus and the future time when he will come again. The following homily for a baptism resulted from approaching this text of Mark from the perspective of Hermes' archetypal world, trusting the images to provide movement, guidance, and a message characterized by metaphorical play. The liturgical event of baptizing several children fits appropriately into the archetypal world of Hermes, rescuer of the child.

Claimed and Named (Mark 1:9-11)

"Why don't you start calling me *Master* Harold,"
      the sixteen year old Hallie says.
With that statement Athol Fugard's play,
      "Master Harold" and the Boys,
            picks up the momentum which will speed it toward its sad
            conclusion.
"Why don't you start calling me *Master* Harold, like Willie," young
      Hallie says to Sam.
Hallie is white; Sam and Willie are black.
The setting is a tea room in Port Elizabeth, South Africa.
Hallie's parents own the tea room; Sam and Willie work there.

"Why don't you start calling me *Master* Harold."
With only eight words, Hallie has begun to move into a new life.

Sam realizes this when he says to Hallie,
    "If you make me say it once,
    I'll never call you anything else again."
But, Hallie insists,
    "Why don't you start calling me *Master* Harold."
A few moments later, Sam does.

A crossroad is reached.
A decision is made.
Hallie has stepped into a river that runs through his country,
    a river named Apartheid.
He has baptized himself with its waters,
    the waters of racism.
Where there had been Hallie and Sam and Willie,
    there is now *Master Harold and the "boys."*

To name is to set in motion.
To name is to move in a certain direction.
The first time I call another friend, spouse, lover
    a shift occurs, a movement toward.
The first time I say to another,
    "stupid," "liar," "enemy,"
    a divide opens between us.

As Jesus stood in the Jordan river, God spoke,
    "You are my beloved son.
    On you my favor rests."
And, with that statement,
    with only ten words,
Jesus of Nazareth began to move into a new life.
Mark opens his gospel by proclaiming the message:
    "The beginning of the gospel of Jesus Christ, the Son of God."
And Mark immediately gives us the basis for this claim.
In Mark's gospel, it is at the Jordan that Jesus first hears himself
    named: "Beloved Son."
And his life moves forward from that particular moment
    away from childhood,
    away from the identity of "the carpenter's son."

He begins to move out and into a journey that will take him to a hill
    named Golgotha where he would once again be named, this
    time by a Roman soldier:
    "Truly, this one was the son of God."

Today something new will be set in motion here.
That life that you mothers felt as it moved in your womb,
That life that you fathers could see growing ever so slowly in your
    beloved's body,
Today that life that in the fullness of its own time moved out into the
    world, into the womb of its larger family of brothers and
    sisters and grandparents and aunts and uncles, and family
    friends,
Today this life will be named anew:
    "Jill Elizabeth, you are my beloved daughter,
    Douglas Peter, you are my beloved son,
    Daniel Gregory, you are my beloved son,
    Lindsey Mari, you are my beloved daughter,
    On each of you my favor rests."

Where shall these lives move?
Where will the spirit drive them?
Like the One in whom they are baptized
    they will know the desert
    and the voice that tempts them to be less than
    "beloved daughter" and "beloved son."
Like the one in whom they are baptized,
    they will walk among rich and poor,
    saints and sinners,
    men and women of different cultures, colors, creeds.

But:
What will they choose to move toward?
    Power? Money? Success?
What will they choose as their guiding star?
    Justice? Compassion? Forgiveness?

Will they move in the awareness of their name:
    "Beloved child,
    Full of grace and favor."

The Spirit hovers this day.
Will it find a permanent home in their hearts?
Much depends on their first dwelling place—
        on you, their parents and godparents,
        on us, this community of faith gathered here.
Through us they will know their identity and calling
        to give life to others,
        to reach out to the lowly and poor,
        to touch the earth with love and respect,
        to walk the way as a disciple.
Through us they will know their family tree—
        Abraham and Sarah,
        Moses and Miriam,
        David and Judith,
        Peter and Paul,
        Martha and Mary
        and all the holy men and women
        who have walked
        the way of the Lord.
Through us they will know Jesus
        as guide and friend,
        as message bearer and mediator,
        as image of Creator God and Spirit God.

Today these children are named and sent forth,
        not alone but with us
        and all who have gone before
        and who will come after:
Today they are claimed and named:
        "Beloved ones,
        Favored ones.
        On you my spirit rests.
        In you my spirit stirs.
        Through you my spirit moves into the world."

7.

Imaginal Preaching: A Brief Excursus and Some Examples

Every occasion of preaching provides an opportunity to sow the biblical images and the images of our tradition. This work has attempted to name ways in which the preacher might think about this important task as an act of the religious imagination. Any image has the capacity to function in a variety of archetypal modalities. I have named only three of them. I would like to offer one instance of taking the lectionary texts assigned to a weekday celebration of the eucharist and briefly indicate how I approached it, taking into account the various archetypal perspectives I have discussed here, and finally deciding on one of them for guiding my use of the day's biblical and liturgical imagery. You will then find some other examples of "imaginal preaching" on various occasions.

An Excursus

A. THE CONTEXT

The occasion for preaching was a daily eucharist celebration at the Washington Theological Union, a school for ministry attended by men and women, vowed religious, laity, and students preparing for the priesthood. It was in the middle of November, a time of year when the semester is drawing to a close and some of the students are taking comprehensive exams, when learning as preparation for a life of ministry can give way to feeling beseiged by academic requirements. The daily liturgy of the eucharist is an oasis when the swirl and whirl can lessen for a few minutes.

The day was also the feast of St. Elizabeth of Hungary. A word about this saint, since this liturgical feast provides its own supply of rich imagery. She was a woman of the thirteenth century, daughter to the king of Hungary, married to Louis, Landgrave of Thuringia, a mother of three, a noblewoman whose less than twenty-four years of life left a legacy that witnessed to caring for the poor, the sick and suffering. On her husband's death, his family tried to have her thrown out of the palace due to her "squandering the royal purse." She is an image of the disciple who has heard the gospel call to care for the least and lowliest.

B. THE BIBLICAL TEXTS

The texts were those assigned to the 33rd Week of the Year, Cycle A: 2 Maccabees 7:1.20-31 and Luke 19:11-28. The first was the account of the mother of the Maccabees witnessing the confrontation between the king and the last of her seven sons. Her own role is central to this account as she encourages her youngest to be faithful to the God of Moses, the God of creation, the God of the Sinai covenant whose statutes and laws the Jewish people were asked to abandon.

The text from Luke is the parable of the pounds, which contains two storylines: the first having to do with a nobleman whose citizens oppose his becoming king and the second with the ten servants entrusted with his money while he is absent. Similar to the parable of the talents in Matthew, this storyline reveals how two of them wisely invested the money while the other buried it. In Luke's presentation, the first narrative reminds us that for those who refuse Jesus' lordship, his coming will be judgment rather than joy, and the second calls his followers to faithfulness and accountability expressed in multiplying what has been given.

C. THE POSSIBILITIES

Image's movement in consciousness is Apollonian when it evokes in listeners an experience of the light, of contact with something that enlightens the mind and elevates the spirit, when it conveys a sense of the holy, and an engagement with mystery. The notes of healing, prophecy, knowledge, and a certain detachment from the world of material reality and matters of feeling also accompany this archetypal realm.

The first reading with its imaginal presentation of the woman and her sons, especially her cool encouragement in facing death, conveys an Apollonian "feel." With its emphasis on heroic fidelity to the law of Moses, the transcending of torture and suffering, and the specific mention of the future restoration by the Creator God, the imaginal world evoked by the text points to the presence of the Holy One. In addition, by attending to the gospel's theme of the nobleman who will return as king to judge those who opposed him and reward those who have served him, these images speak to a prophetic vision of future order and harmony.

On the other hand, from a Hermetic perspective, one can ask how these texts might help a community to continue their journey, what guidance they provide for here and now, how they can be a means of discovering openings through what seems to block us. The figure of the mother might stir up the capacity to endure in the face of overwhelming suffering and tragedy. And the gospel with its servants who make use of what has been entrusted to them offers imagery for the "between time." Christ's parable as featured in Luke is a tale for the traveler, for those who have not yet completed their journey. "What are we to do while we wait for the Lord to return?" is the question underlying this parable. The answer is found in the image of the servants who increased what they had been entrusted with. The context of an eschatological awareness of future judgment or joy also places it within the archetypal framework of Hermes, for as David Miller notes, the realm of eschatology belongs to Hermes, the guide of souls.[1]

But my final decision rested on the juxtaposition of the two women that this day brought together: the mother of the Maccabees and Elizabeth of Hungary. Both can be seen as imaging God in ways that exemplify living embodiment of the gifts of the Spirit. Both in their capacity to function as images of God might loosen the static categories that often are used to speak of God. Both women provide for the community female images of God. So, a framework attentive to the need to integrate female imagery into the more typical male imaging of God led me to feature the two women who could point to She Who Is. I approached the imagery from a Dionysian perspective, looking for its potential to loosen the community from certain set categories, to provide for transformation in its imaging of God, and perhaps even to provide for some an invitation to a more creative way of thinking about God that will involve both a dying and rising. Here is the homily that was given.

D. THE HOMILY

Two Faces of She Who Is

Two women are given special prominence today:
     one known only through her role as the mother of the
     Maccabees;
     the other named Elizabeth, noblewoman,
     wife, and mother.
The first was a follower of the Law of Moses;
     the second, a disciple of Jesus.
Both looked closely at suffering and death,
     and revealed a capacity to respond to it
     that continues to challenge us.
If I were an artist and were to carve them,
     I would work with different materials.

For the mother of the Maccabees, I would choose a white stone.
Only stone could speak of this figure's strength and beauty.
In her we see a courage and faith that borders on the
     incomprehensible,
     so stunning is it that the author is stymied in
     how to speak of her; so he refers to her as being
     "filled with a noble spirit that stirred her
     womanly heart with manly courage."
In this brief analysis, man remains the measure of all good things.

Her own words provide for us a more accurate understanding.
To each son, she spoke:
"It was not I who gave you the breath of life,
     nor I who set in order
     the elements of which each of you is composed.

Therefore, since it is the Creator of the universe who shapes each
    person's beginnings,
      that same Creator will give you back both
      breath and life."
This woman was rooted in God, the source of her being.
She is filled with faith in the Creator God,
    who fashioned her in the
    divine image.
As for the second woman we remember,
    if I were making an image of Elizabeth of Hungary,
    I would choose the warmth of wood.
Her heart could not be limited to the narrow confines that the
    thirteenth century allowed its women.
Married to Louis, Landgrave of Thuringia, at fourteen,
    the mother of three children,
      Throughout her marriage she was a follower of Jesus in her
      love for the poor.
When her husband died in the Crusades after six years of marriage,
    his relatives threw her out of the palace
      because she was squandering all the family riches in
      caring for those in need.
She was a friend to the hungry and the homeless,
    the sick and the stranger.
She was filled with the compassion of the Word made Flesh.

The mother of the Maccabees and the noblewoman of Hungary,
    separated by 1400 years.
Each was unique, as different as stone from wood,
    yet both variations on a theme.
For in each we catch a glimpse of She Who Is.
And from each comes a demand to witness to gifts given
    to us as individuals and to us as a community.

We too are called to witness to She who creates,
    by lives of courage,
      by confronting authority whenever and wherever it is abusive
    and destructive.
We too are called to witness to She who will judge us according to

the gifts given,
by lives of compassion and outreach,
attending to the least and the lowliest.

There is no need to think of "manly courage" filling "womanly hearts"
—just divinity flowing freely through all of human creation.

Some Other Examples

The following are some other homilies written with the goal of featuring images according to one of the archetypal patterns already discussed. In addition to homilies rooted in an image taken from a particular scriptural text, there are some that feature an image of a saint whose feast is being celebrated or an image central to a particular sacramental occasion. But in all these instances my starting point was always with the biblical text and the images it provided, placing these in relation to the particular occasion and community, so that there might be a scriptural interpretation of some aspect of the life of the community.

Homilies developed within the archetypal world of Apollo feature images that attempt to enlighten, sometimes offering a prophetic vision that carries us beyond the here and now; such images try to heal by offering a word that brings balance and harmony to our souls. Their special task is to point us toward an ascent into mystery.

The Presentation of the Lord (Lk 2:22-40)

(This homily, given on the Feast of the Presentation of the Lord in the Temple (February 2) wishes to present two of our ancestors in the faith as figures that continue to utter prophecy for us.)

In this feast celebrating the divine child,
        two senior citizens come before us.
People age differently—
        some grow in fear,
        some in bitterness
        the most fortunate blossom into graciousness.
It's possible all three ran through the hearts of Simeon and Anna.

We don't know how many blows life had dealt them.
We barely know anything about them.
Only one fact is given us—
    that Anna had lost her husband after only seven years.
Did they even know each other?
Maybe a nodding acquaintance—like those old folk who come to
    mass early each morning.

And what was their old age like?
Probably their eyes had dimmed
    and their ears were no longer as sharp.
One thing seems to have held firm:
    they both were attuned to picking up the scent.
Two old watchdogs, waiting:
Simeon, with a readiness to raise the prophetic voice.
Anna, after years of prayer and fasting, a willing accomplice.
Both waiting for an end of waiting.

Much of our lives entails waiting.
And while we wait we begin to wonder.
And the question might blow across our minds without warning:
    What is it all about?
Sometimes it happens at the end of the day.
Sometimes it stretches over a longer period,
    going on for weeks or months.
Or perhaps it comes to some of us as the final companion of life.
And in the silence, a cold shadow might fall across our hearts.
And nothing seems able to dispel it—no vision, no voice,
    at least nothing we can see or hear.
And what we do see and hear brings small comfort.

People continue to kill each other in our city streets.
Our young are looked at with fear and suspicion.
    Anyone else that is different—with distrust, if not hostility.
We need a different way of seeing,
    a fresh vision, a new voice,
    a different scent to pick up on.

Simeon and Anna come and stand next to us.
They could smell God in unexpected places
 like that infant restless in the arms
 of a tired looking young couple.
They are models for us:
 to search out God,
 to wait patiently.
For the light continues to come into the world
 and the glory continues to shine.
The promise still holds:
 the revealing light, the glory of Israel,
 continues to be born and to walk among us.

Easter Week Vesper Service (Jn 3)

The biblical theologian Gerard Sloyan speaks of Nicodemus as
 "a figure of earnest spinelessness."[2]
He sees him as one of the learned who lacked the courage
 to face up to the demands of truth
 for fear of losing his position or social advantage.
That's one way to look at him, I'm sure.
But that's not how I see him.

True, he came to see Jesus at night,
 looking back over his shoulders as he skirted down the side
  streets,
 accompanied by embarrassment for seeking out a teacher from
  Galilee, of all places,
 maybe even with a faint feeling of betrayal of his fellow
  Pharisees who would certainly disapprove of
 this Galilean.
So, he came at night.

But there might have been good reasons.
Perhaps he was carrying an inner darkness that no longer stayed at
 the edge of his consciousness.
Or perhaps it was middle age—he was restless, no longer as certain
 about things as he once had been.

Or there had been too many years of study *about* and not enough
        communion *with* God.
Or maybe there had been a loss—a parent, a spouse, a child.
And so he came at night to the rabbi whose signs spoke of God's
        presence.

And he heard the words of this strange man with the dark eyes.
"You must be born again,
        of the water and wind,
        of the wind which blows where it wills."

You must believe in the Son of Man
        who in being lifted up will draw all into glory,
Then you will know the light.
You will know what is true,
        and do the truth.
Then you will have eternal life.
In the believing is the possessing.

We come in tonight from darkness,
        the darkness of the world.
As chronicled by today's *Washington Post*
        such darkness included:
A front page that spoke of the forty bodies found in Waco.
A metro section that was trying to understand the man arrested for
        driving around with a shotgun the last two months, firing on
        twelve people at blank range.
A style section that "reviewed" the new holocaust museum as an
        abiding testimony to the horror we can commit against each
        other.

We come in tonight with our personal darkness—
        perhaps not as secretive as Nicodemus,
        but, given our median age of late forty-something,
        and given our own questions and struggles,
        a substantial darkness nonetheless.
We come in tonight still trying to live in the truth,

to love God and others,
to be faithful.
We come in hope.

And we are reminded:
that there is a spirit—his—that continues to stir,
that there is a rebirth—in him—that continues to happen,
that there is a light—him—that continues to burn.
May that Spirit blow over us these days.
May the risen Christ burn in, through, for, and with us.
May the loving God from whose womb we have been reborn
continue to nurse us into life.
And so we say:
Amen, alleluia.
He is risen. Alleluia.

Homily for My Stepfather's Funeral (Jn 14:1-6)

St. John's gospel speaks to loss.
If you are feeling in the dark, Jesus tells you that he is the light.
If you feel lost, Jesus tells you that he is the way.
If you feel that death has overwhelmed you, Jesus tells you that he is
the resurrection and the life.
I think my father would have been especially pleased with this
reading where Jesus speaks of the Father as a homeowner with
many mansions.
Not just because my father was a carpenter for a few years after the
Korean war,
or because he worked for the Gas and Electric Company,
servicing homes when people had trouble with their heaters.
But he was a father who appreciated having a home,
who wanted his children to come home for visits,
enjoyed when we got together—and also when we left—
who never tired of telling my brothers and me how important
family was, how we had to stick together.

We gather today to mourn his death and the suddenness of the loss,
but also to profess our faith in the Father whose house has

many mansions,
and in the Son who promises us that he is going to
prepare a place for us, so that where he is, we will also be,
a place where every tear will be wiped away.

We gather together at the eucharist to say thanks to God in the name
of Jesus for the gift of baptismal life given to my father and for
all the gifts that were given to him.
We gather because we know Jesus as the way, the truth and the life.
We gather as a community whose grief is not deeper than its hope.

My father's faith was a simple one, a homey one:
God was the man upstairs, with whom he was on speaking and
trusting terms.
Just last Sunday, he was saying that "When the man upstairs wants
you, that's it. You are on your way home."
(Of course this was also one of the ways he justified ignoring his
doctor's orders.)
But he was a believer in a God he felt at home with.
Years ago, he told me how he would often eat his lunch sitting in the
back of church, before the Blessed Sacrament, and talk things
over with the Lord in his own home.
When I was a child, he would talk to me about my own father, killed
in the war, telling me what a hero my father was, and how he
was sure how God had taken him home.
When I was a thirteen year old, about to leave on the train for the
minor seminary,
he pressed into my hand a medal that he had
carried with him through Korea,
saying it protected him and he was sure it would bring me
safely home.
When I was in college and during the years of theological training,
he would pull me aside, reminding me I always had a home to
come back to.
My father was dedicated to providing a home for his wife and
children.
And so of all the images in John's gospel, the image of the Father's
house with room for all would probably have been his favorite.

My father wasn't a saint;
    he could be exasperating at times.
But he liked people and he always tried to make them feel at home.
And today we can entrust him into the hands of Jesus
    who has prepared a place for him.

Years ago my parents and I and my aunts and uncles went to a
    musical called "The Rothschilds."
It was about the famous banking family.
I remember the end of it.
The father had died, and as the family gathered,
    you heard his voice reciting his will to them.
With only a change in the names, it could serve as my father's will to
    his family:
"To my son Jim, I leave Jerry and Karen and their son Ryan,
    to Jerry and Karen and their son, I leave Bob and Susan and
    their sons Phillip, David, and Luke, and to Bob and Susan
    and their sons, I leave Bill and Louise and their son
    Christopher, and to Bill and Louise and their son, I leave Jim.
And to all of them I leave my fairest jewel, my companion for forty-
    two years, my wife Colette."

God gave us a very good man as a father, friend, companion,
    one who showed us in his own way the way to God.
May we find comfort in knowing that Dad lives now in the Lord.
May we find hope in the resurrection of Jesus,
    trusting in him as the
    way for all of us to one day be together—
    once more at home, this time forever.

Homilies developed within the archetypal perspective of Hermes
look to image's capacity to guide, to speak eloquently, to move us
through the intersections and the seemingly opaque walls that life sets
before us. They offer images that invite us to play, that attempt to surprise and even trick us into awareness, into pondering the mystery that
is friendly, deeply in love with us:

Sts. Philip and James (1 Cor 15:1-8; Jn 14:6-14)

(The following homily was given at a celebration of the eucharist on the feast of Saints Philip and James. The liturgical community was my own religious community composed of seminarians, brothers and priests. I decided to speak in the person of the apostle James, making use particularly of the image of Jesus presented in the gospel.)

Now, it says right here in the first letter of Paul to the Corinthians,
    "Then he appeared to James, then to all the other apostles."
Guess that's why they picked this reading for today.
Only one problem—that's not me.
The James that Paul mentions in his letter—that's not me.
You would think in this day and age with all these biblical people,
    they could get it straight.

You see, there were three of us.
This one here is the brother of Jesus who became bishop of
    Jerusalem.
A strict bird.
Even when they decided to cut out circumcision (pardon the pun),
    he wanted those Gentiles to stay with the Jewish dietary laws.
Then there was James, son of Zebedee,
        the one they call The Greater—
        some say because of his age or his height.
He wished.
Old Jamie was about thirty pounds heavier than the rest of us.
Then there is James, son of Alphaeus.
That's me.
Also called The Lesser,
        because I was thinner than Big Jim,
        and also because I got "lesser mention" in these writings.

You notice they pair me up with Philip.
Between us, Philip was something of a dim bulb.
Remember what you just heard from today's gospel.
Day in and day out Jesus had been going on about how he was in the
        Father and the Father in him and both of them in us.

Now, none of us was sure just exactly what he was getting at.
But we would nod, and hope he'd get on to one of his stories.
But not Philip.
Philip has to go and ask,
    "Show us the Father, Lord."
There was a collective groan from everybody around the table.
Even Jesus stiffened a bit, before explaining very slowly,
"Philip, the one who sees me, sees the Father."
And Philip nods, as if suddenly it's all clear to him.

And that time when we were all out in that deserted spot,
    and all those people scattered about,
    and Jesus asked, "What are we going to do for food?"
You could tell he had something on his mind.
But poor Philip starts counting heads to figure out the cost of bread,
    as if there were a Safeway nearby.
Had the soul of an accountant.
Andrew had the imagination—he spied the boy with two fish and a
    loaf of bread and put two and one together.
The boy gave out what he had;
    then everyone else started sharing.
Turned out there was plenty of food.
But you know all that.

Philip was a good man but very cautious.
Only rash thing he ever did was when Jesus called him.
He got right up from what he was doing and followed.
But there's nothing wrong with caution.
Philip balanced off Peter who didn't know how to spell the word.
And it was Philip who brought Nathaniel to Jesus.
And those Greeks would never have approached Jesus unless we had
    had Philip with us—the Greek name, you see.
Funny how it all works.

We walked with him for three years,
    ran from him once,
    but we soon came back and waited for him.

And then *he* came back to us, with his spirit.
And that's when it all started to take off.

You know, you're not all that much different than we were.
Not all that much to look at.
You might have some academic degrees and that's good
    (there's no virtue in being dumb),
      but what really matters is faith.
Philip had that, and Andrew and Big James and all the rest...and
    me.

Well, now it's your time.
Jesus is still the way, the truth, and the life.
And the best image of God you will ever find.
Believe it.
Speak it.
Live it.
You've got to find your own way to do it.
And there's plenty of challenges out there.
More poor than ever.
More despair.
More hatred and violence.
Whatever way people are taking,
    not too many are taking his.
Someone's got to really do it and be willing to talk about it.
I hope that's you.

Thanksgiving (Mk 5:17-20)

(This homily was one given at a celebration of the eucharist on
Thanksgiving Day. The central figure in this homily is the man possessed by the Gerasene demoniac. All else leads up to and away from
him.)

I was seventeen and visiting that foreign land called Brooklyn.
A group of us, all high school seminarians,
    were going to a place called Lewisohn Stadium
    in an equally mythic location called the Bronx.
Our destination was a pop concert.

It had been raining all day, and that night it graciously stopped.
But thick, heavy clouds were above us.
The soprano was singing one of Rodgers and Hammerstein's
    wonderful songs when it happened.
As if on cue these heavy clouds rolled back over each other,
     revealing a sky with a full moon,
      and a night lavishly sprinkled with stars.
The only possible response was OOOOOOHHH and
    AAAHHHHH!!!
And that sound came from about five thousand people.

More than twenty-five years later
I was an aging student at Northwestern University
    and it was the fourth of July
    and almost 500,000 people were gathered at Soldier Field for
    the fireworks.
The symphony was fighting its way through the 1812 Overture,
    and they finally reached the place for the cannons
    and the night suddenly exploded with fireworks,
    green, red, orange, blue, white—
    streams of fiery light rushing against the night sky.
This time 500,000 people sighed OOOOOHH and AHHHHHHH!!

David Steindl-Rast, a Benedictine monk, says that surprise is the
    beginning of gratitude.
We often think that surprise has to do with things that are
    unpredictable.
But at the deepest level, surprise is recognizing that something is
    somehow gratuitous.
The two moments I have just mentioned were both predictable.
Skies eventually clear after storms
    and people come out on July 4 to see fireworks.
But, for a few seconds, thousands of people were overwhelmed with
    a sense of the gratuitous,
     surrendering to the awareness that
     this marvelous sight was a gift.
And they were on their way to gratitude.

Steindl-Rast says that if we knew enough, everything would be
    predictable and yet gratuitous.

Today we pause as a nation to notice the gratuitous.
Because we are believers, we come to church to do this as a
    community.
Most of the time we hear the gospel about the ten lepers.
They have become the equivalent of the shepherds at Christmas,
        entering our consciousness once a year to call us to gratitude.
But today we heard another gospel suggested for occasions of giving
    thanks—
        the concluding verses of the story of the Gerasene demoniac.
It might seem a strange choice for Thanksgiving.
Yet I think he speaks especially to us and our lives.
The ten lepers remind us to say thanks.
The man liberated from a legion of demons tells us how.

The man, once freed of his demons,
        was aware of the gift that had been given.
He had been in a desperate state,
        living among the dead,
        gashing and tearing his flesh with stones,
        cursing day and night.
He was destructive to himself and others,
        cut off from friends and loved ones.
And he reminds us what life is like without grace,
        that we all have it within ourselves to self-destruct,
        and to turn existence into a living death.

After Jesus comes and restores him—
        both to himself and to his community—
        there is a moment of eloquent simplicity as Mark writes,
        "He wanted to be with Jesus."
Jesus doesn't dismiss his gratitude but channels it.
Jesus makes him the first missionary to the Gentiles.
Jesus says to him:
        "Go home to your family and make it clear to them
        what God in his mercy has done for you."

"Make it clear to them,"
    to your family and neighbors and friends,
    "what God has done for you."
These words can have special resonance in our lives on this day of
    thanksgiving.
By our baptism we are called to be witnesses
    to the good news of the grace and mercy of God.
We are called to live in the awareness of what has been given.

Our lives in Christ call us to be fearless witnesses
    to those with whom we live,
    about what God has done for us.
And whatever helps from our religious tradition,
    whatever helps from our culture,
    whether it is expressed in the language of Augustine,
    or Aquinas, or Lonergan or Rahner,
    or Fox or Greeley or Bly or Star Hawk,
    let us use whatever is at hand to "make it clear
    what God has done for us."

There is a great need to know what God has done and can do,
    especially through other human beings.
Sometimes we drown in only seeing what evil can do.
Elie Wiesel was being interviewed by Bill Moyers recently.
He was speaking about what the Nazis did during those fateful years
    of the holocaust.
He noted how they shrank the world for the Jewish people:
    from their being inhabitants of the world
    to being confined to one nation
    then to a city
    then to a ghetto,
    a house,
    a room
    and, finally, to a few inches of space in a concentration camp.
And, in doing this, they shrank the human person:
    from a person
    to a number
    to ash.

This is what we humans are capable of,
     and this must never be forgotten.

And such horror has not ended with the Nazis—
     we cannot forget the blood of Vietnam or of Iraq,
     and now Bosnia and Somalia,
     and tomorrow....
We are called to make it clear what God has done,
     what God continues to do,
     not just for us personally but for us as a community.

Mark concludes this tale by saying that the man went out
     proclaiming through the ten cities what God had done.
This could be seen as hyperbole on Mark's part,
     or even as appropriate enthusiasm of one delivered from a
     legion of demons.
But perhaps it was the only response possible
     from one who had become aware that *all* are family,
     not simply the few bound by birth or friendship.

Today's national feast can easily be banalized—
     pretty pilgrims and new age native Americans gathered over
     seventeenth century drinks and finger food.
But remember that these were two peoples who each suspected the
     other was barely human.
The image of two suspicious groups, sharing food
     and, for a few moments, realizing
     that they were not totally unlike or unrelated
     but actually linked—such is the beginning of family,
     and the beginning of gratitude for the gratuitous.

A moon in full splendor can evoke an OOOOOHH.
A sky full of fireworks can call forth an AHHHH.
But the realization that comes to us in faith,
     that we are family,
     that we are one in God, in Jesus Christ, in the Spirit,
     should nudge us to the simplest of all responses:
     Thank you. Thank you. Thank you.

An Advent Homily (Mt 1:18-24)

In these final days of Advent,
> the gospel readings for the celebration of daily eucharist
> place before us those I call "the Christmas people."

We hear once again the listing of the family tree of Jesus recorded in
> Matthew,

We hear about Zechariah and Elizabeth,
> about Mary,
> and, tonight, about Joseph.

Every year we are reintroduced to the Christmas people.

Have you ever wondered what purpose they serve in our lives?

Last weekend I reread Barbara Robinson's wonderful little book,
> *The Best Christmas Pageant Ever.*

It's the story of the Herdman kids—
> Ralph, Imogene, Ollie, Leroy, Claude, and Gladys.

The Herdmans are the absolutely worst kids in the history of the
> world.

They lie, steal, smoke cigars, talk dirty, hit little kids, cuss their
> teachers, and take the name of the Lord in vain.

The story is what happens when the Herdmans volunteer themselves
> for the key roles in the church Christmas pageant one year.

When the people of the parish hear about it, they are appalled,
> because the Herdmans were the closest thing to criminals and
> they were going to represent the best and most beautiful.

The power of the story is what happens as these children begin to
> take on their roles.

At the first rehearsal it is clear that they have never heard the
> Christmas story.

They knew that Christmas was Jesus' birthday but everything else
> was new to them—the shepherds, the wise men, the angels,
> and the inn.

And so they begin to shape their roles.

They can't accept that Joseph and a pregnant Mary can't get a room
> in the inn, and they want Ralph who is Joseph to burn it down
> or at least chase the innkeeper into the next county.

And when Gladys comes on the rehearsal scene as the angel of glad
  tidings she goes through the rest of the angelic chorus
  whacking one angel after another.
The three kings as played by Leroy, Claude and Ollie want to end the
  pageant by stringing up Herod.
And Imogene is playing Mary like Mrs. Santoro, a loud and bossy
  fat lady with a skinny husband who yells and hollers a lot and
  hugs her kids and slaps them around.

But while they start off shaping these roles to their personalities,
  eventually, the roles begin to shape them.
And the night of the performance,
    when all the people have filled the church
    and all the rest of the kids dressed as shepherds
    and angels are singing carols, when it comes time
    for Imogene and Ralph to appear they look like two
    refugees, standing there startled, like that first couple
    probably was.
And when Gladys appears as the angel and shouts,
    "Hey, unto you a child is born!"
    she hollers it as if it were the best news you ever heard
    and you believe it.
And when Ollie, and Ralph and Claude come in as the kings,
    they don't have gold, frankincense and myrrh as their gifts, but
    the baked ham that their family was given for Christmas
    dinner.
In the end their roles shape them.

There is a wisdom in the tradition of having Christmas pageants.
And a similar wisdom guides the church's decision to have certain
  gospels read for the last week of Advent,
    presenting us with the Christmas people.
The hope is they might shape us.
Today the spotlight is on Joseph.

He never talks in scripture.
Never has any of the punch lines.
This is probably his biggest moment.

And even here, he doesn't get a word in,
>being upstaged by an angel.
But this moment offers us a role to grow into,
>because it lays out one way that Christ
>continues to come into the world.

Joseph is described as a just man.
He was dedicated to Torah,
>listening and being obedient to the law of the Lord.
The law of Leviticus demanded that a woman who became pregnant
>was to be set aside so as to protect the sanctity of marriage.
And so when Mary was found to be pregnant he decided to divorce
her.
But Joseph also heard Torah's call to care for the defenseless.
And so he decided to divorce her quietly.

We see Joseph presented as one who keeps the law as it was known
>and handed down to him.
But there is more.
He is also presented as one who fulfills the will of God as it *becomes*
>known to him.
And so, when an angel comes in a dream,
>Joseph listens to the voice that it speaks.
Thus he becomes one who fulfills the law that is spoken to the heart.
In doing this, Joseph enables the words of the prophet Isaiah to come
>to fulfillment:
>>"The virgin shall be with child.
>>and give birth to a son,
>>and they shall call him Emmanuel."
In this, Joseph is held up to us
>not only as one who tries to fulfill the words of the law,
>but also as one whose openness leads to fulfilling the words
>of the prophet.

We are called to grow into the role of Joseph.
We do this
>when we attend to what is holy as it is handed down to us,
>and when we do our best to defend the weak and helpless.

We do this
>   when we attend to that voice that calls us to go beyond the ·
>   accepted or imposed limits,
>   when we are open to God's ability to do new things,
>   so that God might be born once again into our world.

All of us can play Joseph in our own way,
>   but to the degree that we come to understand him,
>   we can say that Joseph will shape us.

And, as a community, the role of Joseph can teach us something very
>   important:
That Emmanuel comes
>   not only when we are obedient to the traditions we have come
>   to know as "the law of God,"
>   but also through the voice of the angel that continues to speak
>   to us,
>   calling us to attend to the poor in our midst,
>   to defend those who have been abused,
>   to work against any discrimination that diminishes
>   the human dignity of others.
Only then will others know that God is truly Emmanuel,
God-with-us.

By Way of an Epilogue

Images mediate encounter. Through our images we encounter the "other." Often the "other" is part of our world—other people, places, things. Sometimes that "other" is a hidden aspect of ourselves, as in the images that come to us in dreams and fantasies. Images mediate the past and the future. And images mediate the divine. This work has attempted to call attention to the images that we preachers offer to our people, especially the images of scripture entrusted to us by those who have preceded us to hand on to our own and the next generation.

Because we are bombarded by so many images in the course of the day, we tend to filter out many of them, attending only to those which demand our attention. Our familiarity with the biblical texts can easily lead us to take on such an attitude toward them. We move toward "meaning" in terms of the concept or the idea found within a text, then look elsewhere to find the images that will hold attention. Certainly image begets image, and the images of the tradition serve as a catalyst for gathering other images about them. But the first step in any kind of imaginal preaching is to attend to what is at hand, to honor, respect and love those images to be found in the Bible which can continue to be such an enriching part of our liturgical and spiritual lives.

Leland Roloff has written of the importance of *consent* in an act of performance. A preacher *consents* to the images that have been entrusted to him, whether those handed down from the past or those that have "come" to him in the creative process. Roloff observes that the nature of this *consent* can be seen as "a grace, a capability of mind, a largeness, if you will, by which something can enter, can infuse, can ignite a quality of spirit that will lead [one] out of ignorance into another revelation."[1]

Such consent is needed from the preacher. He or she must have that gracious ability that allows the image to enter and work itself into his or her thoughts, feelings, imagination, and then is offered to the people the preacher serves.

Our work here has been concerned with texts that are predominantly imaginal. But images can be found in all texts, either as the context in which the text is located or within the very words themselves. It can be fascinating to discover the images that are hidden within words. When Hillman calls us to see angels as inherent within words, seeing words as independent carriers of soul between people, he is calling us to attend to words as the place where thought, image, and feeling converge.

The imaginal world is the world of soul. As such it can carry us into a variety of archetypal presences and their perspectives. We have considered three of them in this work, those of Apollo, Dionysus, and Hermes. These three archetypal realms each have distinct qualities. The same image can be crafted in ways appropriate to each mode so as to function in different ways in the consciousness of listeners. I chose to work with only three of the archetypal powers and their worlds. Why these three? Because they are the ones that I have lived with over the years. Perhaps it is more accurate to say that these are the three that have visited me.

I know these three modalities do not exhaust the ways in which images can function in preaching. There are also the female archetypal powers that operate in the consciousness of both men and women. Figures like Hestia, the goddess of the hearth, speaks of the images that center us; Aphrodite, of the sensuous images that woo us; Artemis, of the virginal images that entice and elude and call us to freedom; and Athene, of the images that turn us toward the good of the *polis*, the political order, the common good. There is further work to be done here.

In the past the gods and goddesses have been seen as merely the discarded figures of Greece and Rome's polytheistic cultic life; the Renaissance and the Romantics looked again and found new richness in the worlds they represented. Now the perspective offered by archetypal psychology encourages their acceptance into the imaginal sphere of soul as a way to think about how images settle and bear fruit in the imaginations of our community. Jung thought that the archetypes were bringers of protection and salvation. In this way, we might see them as participations in the ongoing work of the Holy Spirit. And the three figures considered here are three ways to name manifestations of the Spirit's continuing efforts to bring life through our spoken words.

Archetypal psychology's contribution to the work of preachers includes the insistence that soul is without end; its depths cannot be measured. The task of the preacher is to offer images that awaken the souls in the community and the community soul. The preacher's love for the image can be one of the greatest gifts communicated to the community. The child of Eros and Psyche is Joy. When joy is continually being born in a community through the power and beauty of its imaginal life, there is cause for praise and thanksgiving.

Notes

Introduction

1. James Hillman, *Insearch* (Irving, Texas: Spring, 1979), p. 108.

1. The Imaginal World and Preaching

1. Neil Postman and Camille Paglia, "She Wants Her TV! He Wants His Book!" *Harpers* (March, 1991), p. 54.
2. Thomas Troeger, "Homiletics as Imaginative Theology," *Homiletic* XII (1987) No. 2, p. 27.
3. John Coleman, *An American Strategic Theology* (New York: Paulist, 1982), p. 158.
4. Ibid.
5. Robert Bellah et al., *Habits of the Heart* (Berkeley: University of California, 1985).
6. Mircea Eliade, *Images and Symbols: Studies in Religious Symbolism* (New York: Sheed, 1961), p. 11.
7. Brian Friel, *Translations* (New York: Samuel French, 1981), p. 81.
8. Thomas G. Long, *The Witness of Preaching* (Louisville: Westminster/John Knox Press, 1989), p. 24.
9. Walter M. Abbott, S.J., *The Documents of Vatican II*, "Constitution on the Sacred Liturgy," #35,2 (New York: Guild Press, 1966), pp. 149-150. Emphasis mine.
10. Abbott (ed.), *The Documents of Vatican II*, "The Decree on the Ministry and Life of Priests," #4, p. 538.
11. Richard A. Jensen, *Thinking in Story: Preaching in a Post-literate Age* (Lima, Ohio: CSS, 1993), p. 73.

12. *The Canons and Decrees of the Council of Trent*, trans. and introduced by Rev. H.J. Schroeder, O.P. (Rockfield: Tan, Inc., 1978), p. 26.
13. Abbott, "Constitution on Sacred Liturgy, #52, p. #155.
14. William J. Carl III, *Preaching Christian Doctrine* (Philadelphia: Fortress, 1984), p. 3.
15. For a more extended treatment of the preacher as pastor, see Thomas G. Long's *The Witness of Preaching*, pp. 30-36. The image of the preacher as pastor can be related both to the preacher as teacher and to the preacher as interpreter (to be discussed shortly), insofar as both are attentive to the needs of the listeners.
16. Pope Paul VI, *On Evangelization in the Modern World* (Washington, D.C.: United States Catholic Conference, 1975), p. 28.
17. Ibid.
18. Thomas G. Long, *The Witness of Preaching* (Louisville: Westminster/John Knox Press, 1989).
19. Ibid., p. 43.
20. Ibid., p. 44.
21. Abbott, "Constitution on the Sacred Liturgy," #52, p. 155.
22. Austin Flannery, O.P., ed., *Vatican Council II: The Conciliar and Post Conciliar Documents*, "General Instruction on the Roman Missal," #9 (Northport: Costello, 1975), p. 164.
23. Bishops' Committee on Priestly Life and Ministry, *Fulfilled in Your Hearing: The Homily in the Sunday Assembly* (Washington, D.C.: USCC, 1982), p. 29.
24. Edmund Steimle, Charles Rice, and Morris Niedenthal, *Preaching the Story* (Philadelphia: Fortress, 1980), p. 34.
25. See Robert P. Waznak, *Sunday after Sunday: Preaching the Homily as Story* (New York: Paulist, 1983); Wayne Bradley Robinson (ed.), *Journeys Toward Narrative Preaching* (New York: Pilgrim, 1990); Richard L. Thulin, *The "I" of the Sermon* (Philadelphia: Fortress, 1989); Eugene L. Lowry, *How To Preach a Parable: Designs for Narrative Sermons* (Nashville: Abingdon, 1989); and Paul Scott Wilson, *Imagination of the Heart: New Understandings in Preaching* (Nashville: Abingdon, 1988). For a very helpful summary and critique of some of the key spokespersons in narrative preaching, see Richard Eslinger's *A New*

Hearing: Living Options in Homiletic Method (Nashville: Abingdon, 1987).

26. Garrett Green, *Imagining God: Theology and the Religious Imagination* (San Francisco: Harper and Row, 1989).

27. Rubem A. Alves, *The Poet, the Warrior, the Prophet* (London: SCM Press, 1990), p. 39.

28. *Fulfilled in Your Hearing*, p. 25.

29. Elizabeth Achtemeier, *Creative Preaching* (Nashville: Abingdon, 1981), p. 24.

30. Thomas Troeger, *Creating Fresh Images for Preaching* (Valley Forge: Judson, 1982), p. 30.

31. See Walter Brueggemann, *Finally Comes the Poet* (Philadelphia: Fortress, 1989), especially pp. 79-110.

32. William F. Lynch, S.J., "The Life of Faith and Imagination: Theological Reflection in Art and Literature," *Thought* 57 (March, 1982), p. 11.

33. One of the most stimulating and important works to deal with the naming of God is Elizabeth A. Johnson's *She Who Is: The Mystery of God in Feminist Theological Discourse* (New York: Crossroad, 1992).

34. Mark Searle, "Images and Worship," *The Way* 24 (April, 1984), p. 108.

35. *Fulfilled in Your Hearing*, p. 20.

2. The Soul's Language:
Images and the Archetypal World of James Hillman

1. *A Blue Fire: Selected Writings by James Hillman*, introduced and edited by Thomas Moore (New York: Harper and Row, 1989), p. 15.

2. Excerpt found in *A Blue Fire*, pp. 43-44.

3. Ibid.

4. Hillman, *Archetypal Psychology: A Brief Account* (Dallas: Spring, 1983), p.16.

5. Ibid.

6. Thomas Moore, *Care of the Soul: A Guide for Cultivating Depth and Sacredness in Everyday Life* (New York: HarperCollins, 1992), p. 5.

7. Hillman, *Archetypal Psychology*, pp. 16-17.

8. Ibid., p. 27.

9. Hillman, "Anima Mundi," *Spring*, 1982, p. 87.

10. James Hillman, *Archetypal Psychology*, p. 53.

11. Ibid., p. 13.

12. Ibid., p. 169.

13. Hillman, *Re-Visioning Psychology* (New York: Harper and Row, 1975), p. 167.

14. Ibid., p. 37.

15. Hillman, *The Thought of the Heart*, Eranos Lectures #2 (Dallas: Spring, 1981), p. 2.

16. Walter Vogels, *Reading and Preaching the Bible: A New Semiotic Approach* (Wilmington: Michael Glazier, 1986), p. 150.

17. From *A Blue Fire*, pp. 55-56.

18. Hillman, "An Inquiry into Image," *Spring*, 1977, p. 81.

19. James Hillman, with Laura Pozzo, *Inter Views* (New York: Harper Colophon, 1983), p. 81.

20. Hillman, *Re-Visioning Psychology*, p. 9.

3. Eros and the Homiletic Process

1. James Hillman, *Inter Views*, p. 178.

2. Quoted in Russell A. Lockhart, *Words as Eggs: Psyche in Language and Clinic* (Dallas: Spring, 1983), p. 113.

3. The myth of Eros and Psyche is found in Apuleius' *The Golden Ass*, trans. by Robert Graves (New York: Farrar, Strauss, and Giroux, 1984), pp. 95-143. Other versions can be found in A.R. Hope Moncrieff, *Classic Myth and Legend* (New York: Wm. A. Wise and Co., 1934), pp. 369-383; and Erich Neumann, *Amor and Psyche: The Psychic Development of the Feminine; A Commentary on the Tale by Apuleius* (Princeton: Princeton University Press, 1956), pp. 3-53. The version in this text is indebted to each of these.

4. Neumann, op. cit.; Marie Louise Von Franz, *A Psychological Interpretation of the Golden Ass of Apuleius* (Irving: Spring,

1980). See also Jean Houston's discussion in *The Search for the Beloved: Journeys in Mythology and Sacred Psychology* (Los Angeles: Jeremy P. Tarcher, Inc., 1987), pp. 151-188.

5. See James Hillman, *The Myth of Analysis*, Chapter 1 (New York: Harper, 1972), pp. 11-113.

6. Aldo Carotenuto, *Eros and Pathos: Shades of Love and Suffering*, trans. by Charles Nopar (Toronto: Inner City, 1989), pp. 15, 19.

7. Quote by Mark Searle, in "Images and Worship," *The Way* 24 (April, 1984), p. 109.

8. Von Franz, pp. 92-93.

9. For this text, I turned to the following commentaries for their insight: Fred B. Craddock, *Luke*, Interpretation Series (Louisville: John Knox, 1990); Luke Timothy Johnson, *The Gospel of Luke*, Sacra Pagina Series (Collegeville: Liturgical, 1991); Eugene LaVerdiere, S.S.S., *Luke*, New Testament Message (Wilmington: Michael Glazier, 1983).

10. Von Franz, p. 98.

11. Alves, The Poet, *The Warrior, The Prophet*, pp. 46-47.

12. Carl G. Jung, *Memories, Dreams, Reflections*, trans. by Aniela Jaffe (New York: Vintage, 1965), p. 353.

13. James Hillman, *The Myth of Analysis: Three Essays in Archetypal Psychology* (New York: Harper, 1978), p. 70.

4. Imaginal Preaching and Apollo

1. Charles Boer (trans.), "Hymn to Delian Apollo," *The Homeric Hymns* (Irving: Spring, 1979), p. 149.

2. Christine Downing, *Gods in Our Midst, Mythological Images of the Masculine: A Woman's View* (New York: Crossroad, 1993), p. 91.

3. Arianna Stassinopoulos and Roloff Beny, *The Gods of Greece* (New York: Harry N. Abrams, 1983), p. 53.

4. See Downing, pp. 85-102. Toward the end of her essay on Apollo, she writes of her relationship to the god and his world: "...it seems signally important that I acknowledge the struggle for autonomy, for clarity, for objectivity as something I participate in, something I bless and love, but also something that I

know can take over and separate me from other aspects of my being I also value" (pp. 100-101).

5. Walter Otto, *The Homeric Gods*, trans. Moses Hadas (London: Thames and Hudson, 1979), p. 78.
6. Hillman, "Peaks and Vales," in *The Puer Papers* (Irving: Spring, 1979), p. 58.
7. Rollo May, *The Courage to Create* (New York: W.W. Norton, 1975), pp 106-107.
8. Pedro Lain Entralgo, *The Therapy of the Word in Classical Antiquity*, trans. L.J. Rather and John M. Sharp (New Haven: Yale, 1970).
9. Ibid., p. 123.
10. Ibid.
11. Walker Percy, "The Diagnostic Novel," *Harper's* (June, 1986), p. 41.
12. James Hillman, *Inter Views: Conversations with Laura Pozzo on Psychotherapy, Biography, Love, Soul, Dreams, Work, Imagination, and the State of the Culture* (New York: Harper, 1983), p. 25.
13. Flannery O'Connor, *Mystery and Manners* (New York: Farrar, Straus and Giroux, 1969), p. 72.
14. Madeleine L'Engle, *Walking on Water: Reflections on Faith and Art* (Wheaton: Harold Shaw, 1980), Chapters 1 and 2, pp. 11-50.

5. Imaginal Preaching and Dionysus

1. Stassinopoulos and Beny, *The Gods of Greece*, p. 97.
2. Jean Shinoda Bolen, *Gods in Everyman: A New Psychology of Men's Lives and Loves* (San Francisco: Harper and Row, 1989), p. 254.
3. Peter Shaffer, *Equus* (New York: Avon, 1975). All quotations are taken from this edition.
4. Ibid., p. 88.
5. Ibid., pp. 87-88.
6. Ibid., pp. 123-124.
7. Walter Otto, *Dionysus: Myth and Cult* (Dallas: Spring, 1981), p. 143.
8. Ibid., pp. 136-137.

9. Plato, *Phaedrus*, trans. by W.C. Helmbold and W.G. Rabinowitz (Indianapolis: Bobbs-Merrill, 1981), #265, p. 54.

10. Downing, *Gods in Our Midst*, p. 73.

11. James Hillman, *The Myth of Analysis* (New York: Harper and Row, 1972), p. 258.

12. Ibid., p. 259.

13. Ibid., p. 282.

14. Mary Catherine Hilkert, OP, "Sunday Preaching from a Woman's Point of View," *The Good News Letter*, Easter, 1993, p. 5.

15. Mary Gordon, "Coming to Terms with Mary," *Commonweal* (January 15, 1982), p. 11.

16. For instance, see Naomi R. Goldenberg's *Changing of the Gods: Feminism and the End of Traditional Religions* (Boston: Beacon, 1979), pp. 75-78. Goldenberg speaks of Mary as one who has "certainly been desexed by Christian tradition.... Mary has been castrated by popes, cardinals, priests, and theologians, by all who fear the sexual and emotional power of natural womanhood." Goldenberg is suspicious of all efforts to consider Mary as the "liberated woman of Christianity" (pp. 75-76).

6. Imaginal Preaching and Hermes

1. Athol Fugard, *The Road to Mecca* (New York: Theater Communications, 1987), p. 67.

2. Ibid., p. 63.

3. Ibid., p. 65.

4. James Hillman, "Notes on Opportunism," *The Puer Papers* (Irving: Spring, 1979), p. 163.

5. For a succinct treatment of the three components of the state of liminality, see "Religious Celebrations," by Victor and Edith Turner, in *Celebration: Studies in Festivity and Ritual*, ed. by Victor Turner (Washington: Smithsonian, 1982), pp. 201-206.

6. Of particular interest in linking play with the archetypal world of Hermes is Turner's eloquent understanding of play articulated in terms that could be used to describe Hermes himself: "Play is a light-winged, light-fingered skeptic, a Puck between the day world of Theseus and the night world of Oberon, putting into question the cherished assumptions of both hemispheres, both

worlds. There is no sanctity in play; it is irreverent and is protected in the world of power struggles by its apparent irrelevance
and clown's garb." *The Anthropology of Performance* (New
York: PAJ, 1986), p. 170.

7. Frederick Buechner, *Wishful Thinking* (San Francisco: Harper
and Row, 1973), pp. 43, 79.

8. These quotes are taken from *Peculiar Treasures: A Biblical
Who's Who* (San Francisco: Harper and Row, 1979). For anoth-
er work by Buechner that provides imaginative treatment of bib-
lical stories and characters, see *Telling the Truth: The Gospel as
Tragedy, Comedy and Fairy Tale* (San Francisco: Harper and
Row, 1977).

9. Amanda Cross, *Sweet Death, Kind Death* (New York: Avon,
1980), p. 22.

10. Arianna Stassinopoulos and Roloff Beny, *The Gods of Greece*
(New York: Harry N. Abrams, 1983), p. 197.

11. See Mary Ann Tolbert, "How the Gospel of Mark Builds
Character," *Interpretation* (October, 1993), footnote 12, p. 357.

7. Imaginal Preaching:
A Brief Excursus and Some Examples

1. David Miller, *The New Polytheism* (New York: Harper and Row,
1974), p. 71.

2. Gerard Sloyan, *John* (Atlanta: John Knox, 1988), p. 44.

By Way of an Epilogue

1. Leland Zahner-Roloff, "Performer, Performing, Performance—
Towards a Psychologicalization of Theory," unpublished manuscript, p. 3.

Index of Names
and Subjects